Geopolitical Cyber Threat Intelligence

ROBIN DIMYANOGLU

ISBN: 979-8-33-789164-4

CONTENTS

Robin Dimyanoglu

CONTENTS

Geopolitical Cyber Threat Intelligence

...to my beloved wife, whose support and love made this journey possible.

Foreword

"Geopolitical Cyber Threat Intelligence" is a book I've tailored specifically for us, cyber threat intelligence analysts. During our daily work, we often find ourselves at the intersection of cyber activities and geopolitics, trying to make sense of these attacks in a broader context. We need a deeper understanding of how cyber operations intersect with national policies, and this book delivers just that.

The content is structured to improve our understanding of how cyber capabilities are used as enablers in the broader pursuit of geopolitical objectives. It's designed to help CTI analysts understand the factors that shape national policies and the dynamics that might escalate into international tensions or conflicts.

Before we dive into the book, I need to clarify a few points about its content. First off, if you're familiar with social sciences literature, you've likely noticed that scholars addressing the same issues might use vastly different analytical methods. For instance, when analyzing Iran's foreign policy, one analyst might focus on cultural and ideological factors, while another could prioritize Iran's security needs. A third might use the history of imperialism and a critique of the international system to provide explanations. This humorously suggests that in a room with three social scientists, you might find four different opinions.

It's important to acknowledge that all these viewpoints are valid to some extent. In other words, no single analytical approach is absolutely correct because social structures have a non-deterministic nature. Unlike natural sciences or engineering, the methodologies applied in social sciences may not consistently yield the same level of success across different scenarios. For example, a model used to predict coups in Latin America during the Cold War might not work as well for coups in the Middle East.

In this book, I've given preference to certain factors over others in my analysis methods, reflecting my own presuppositions. Although I consider political, socio-cultural, and technological aspects, I argue that the most influential factors in state policies are economy and security.

Particularly after the industrial revolution, which greatly boosted production efficiency, states have sought economic prosperity through industrial production, competing fiercely to secure essential resources like oil and minerals at the lowest costs and to sell their products in the widest possible markets.

You will notice that the discussions of state policies in this book predominantly revolve around these economic and security elements. However, I do not claim that this approach is the sole or best way to analyze them. I encourage readers to explore and engage with other analytical methods that emphasize different factors.

The second point I want to discuss concerns the case studies featured in this book. Most examples pertain to the Middle East, reflecting my background as a Turkish author more acquainted with this region's politics. An important side effect to consider is that my analysis may overly reflect Middle Eastern dynamics. Despite my best efforts to avoid 'overfitting'—a term from machine learning—, my personal experiences inevitably shape my perspective and interpretation of events. Readers might find it beneficial to reevaluate the prioritized factors when applying these methods to other regions, like East Asia or Latin America.

Finally, the case studies in this book are not based on exhaustive research but are used primarily to illustrate the analytical methods. Therefore, the insights derived from this book should not be directly implemented in decision-making processes. Institutions should adapt these analyses according to their unique factors and integrate the results into decision-making only after thorough evaluation.

With these points made clear, let's start our exploration of geopolitical cyber threat intelligence. I hope you find it both enjoyable and insightful. Happy reading!

How Intelligence Agencies Work

Intelligence agencies globally serve their respective states' short, medium, and long-term policy objectives. They assist these states in the process of making informed decisions by providing information on immediate and strategic issues to the decision-makers. Cyber espionage is increasingly used by intelligence agencies due to its cost-effectiveness and scalability. In the field of cyber threat intelligence, we frequently observe such activities, especially in reports concerning Advanced Persistent Threats. However, simply knowing the common targets of APTs offers limited help in predicting their attacks. A more effective approach is to understand various intelligence collection needs and incorporate these insights into our own threat model.

The intelligence requirements of states are largely influenced by their pursued policies. Every nation aims to achieve political, economic, and sometimes military advantages on the international stage. Therefore, these specific aspirations shape their medium and long-term political, economic, and military goals. By examining a particular country, its primary interests in political, economic, and military matters can reveal its goals and hence its likely intelligence needs. This understanding allows us to identify potential intelligence targets in different countries, sectors, and organizations.

An example is China's ongoing commercial expansion strategy, which has been in effect since the mid-2010s. This strategy includes initiatives like the Belt and Road Initiative[1] and the Made in China 2025 plan[2]. China's goal is to use its greatly increased manufacturing capacity to gain economic and political influence. The nation is focusing on shifting its manufacturing towards high-tech production and is actively engaging in diplomatic efforts to build trade relationships.

The key sectors and trade targets under this policy are outlined in China's strategic documents. Regarding intelligence needs, China might focus on:

1. Intellectual property and technical information that could benefit Chinese companies in high-tech manufacturing.
2. Political intelligence that supports China's diplomatic efforts to expand its trade networks.

---

[1] https://www.ebrd.com/what-we-do/belt-and-road/overview.html

[2] https://www.plattform-i40.de/IP/Redaktion/EN/Downloads/Publikation/China/MIC2025_factsheet.pdf?__blob=publicationFile&v=1

To predict the potential targets of Chinese intelligence services based on the aforementioned policies, we could consider the following questions:

1. What high-tech products is China looking to manufacture in the future?
2. Who are the key players (countries and companies) currently producing these high-tech products China wants to manufacture?
3. Which sectors is China focusing on to boost its foreign trade?
4. Who are China's biggest competitors in these target sectors?
5. Which countries is China looking to make new trade agreements?
6. In what sectors is China planning to increase its trade through these new agreements?

Countries have a variety of intelligence needs, which over time have led to the development of different specialized intelligence gathering disciplines[3]. These specializations often arise from the unique characteristics of the environment where intelligence is gathered. For instance, signals intelligence evolved from the need to process electromagnetic signals for intelligence collection. Another factor is the need for expertise in certain topics which the intelligence will be collected about.

Today, the most common types of intelligence operations can be categorized into seven main groups:

Political Intelligence: This involves gathering information about political trends, policies, and actions of governments, political groups, or leaders. It's crucial for

---

[3] https://en.wikipedia.org/wiki/List_of_intelligence_gathering_disciplines

understanding the political landscape, potential legislation, diplomatic relations, and decision-making processes.

Economic Intelligence: This focuses on collecting and analyzing information related to the global economy, trade, industry trends, and economic policies of countries. It's used to understand market dynamics, competitors, and economic threats or opportunities.

Military Intelligence: Concerned with information about the capabilities, intentions, and activities of foreign militaries. This includes understanding their strength, strategy, weaponry, troop movements, and defense systems.

Financial Intelligence: This involves gathering data on financial transactions, monetary policies, and the financial health of entities (such as states, corporations, and individuals). It's crucial for the detection of financial crimes like money laundering, terrorism financing, and fraud.

Technical Intelligence: This intelligence focuses on foreign advancements in science and technology. It covers emerging technologies, scientific research, and innovations across various fields like biotech, aerospace, and computing. Crucial for staying ahead in technology, it helps in anticipating technological threats and informs strategic R&D planning.

Geospatial Intelligence: It involves analyzing imagery and geospatial information to describe, assess, and visually depict physical features and geographically referenced activities on the Earth. This can include mapping, charting, and satellite imagery.

Communications Intelligence: This is the gathering of intelligence through the interception and analysis of foreign communications. This includes understanding foreign communication networks, decoding encrypted messages, and analyzing communication patterns.

A significant portion of cyber espionage activities stem from political, economic, and military intelligence efforts, but it's possible to see all these types of intelligence activities being carried out in the cyber realm. Different intelligence disciplines cater to the varying policy areas of countries. Understanding these needs aids in identifying how our organization's assets can potentially overlap with these requirements, guiding us in cyber defense planning.

Comparison: Strategic vs. Tactical Collection Targets

Intelligence needs vary in their level of importance and urgency. Some intelligence supports long-term strategies, while others address immediate, time-sensitive situations. For example, the intelligence needed during a military conflict is much more immediate compared to that needed for planning foreign trade over five years. Different targeting and collection methods are employed in order to cater to these different needs. In this section, we will name them as **Strategic collection** and **Tactical collection** efforts. These should not be confused with the broader concepts of strategic and tactical intelligence.

Strategic Collection: If a target can provide information valuable for long-term goals, or can provide information the agency is in constant need, or can satisfy multiple intelligence requirements simultaneously, then it is likely to be a focus of strategic collection efforts. Such targets will likely face persistent intrusion attempts unless an alternative information source is found by the intelligence agency. They might also be defined as permanent intelligence targets. Typical examples of these types of targets are government departments and key political figures.

An intelligence target can be classified as **strategic** when:

1. It is capable of supplying information that supports long-term policies.
2. It can fulfill several intelligence requirements simultaneously.
3. It can offer information that an agency consistently requires.

Targeting is expected to be persistent, adaptive, and long term, but less likely to employ advanced, event-based capabilities (e.g: zero-day exploits).

Tactical Collection: If the intelligence need is immediate, (e.g: during diplomatic crises, law enforcement investigations, or active conflicts) or if the information is of a tactical nature, then the target is likely to be a focus of tactical collection efforts. Depending on the urgency and criticality of the information needed, advanced event-based capabilities like zero-day exploits might be used. This is less common in strategic collection, as the need for information is long-term and can often be met from multiple sources.

An intelligence target can be classified as **tactical** when:

1. A target may be capable of fulfilling intelligence needs that are immediate and critical.
2. A target may provide information that an agency is unable to obtain through alternative sources.

Targeting is expected to be persistent and adaptive, and more likely to employ advanced, event-based capabilities.

Understanding Nation State Policies

The idea that states, much like corporations, establish goals for themselves over short, medium, and long terms might be surprising to some. In their strategic planning, states are obliged to maintain a balance across several key factors, including security, economic growth, and social welfare. This process is further influenced by the geographical situation of the state and the conditions of the countries with which it interacts. For instance, a country typically focused on foreign trade may be compelled to shift its priority to security in response to a civil war in a neighboring nation.

The widely accepted belief is that economic growth leads to societal welfare. Thus, every state, in one way or another, strives for economic development and shapes its policies accordingly. Essentially, it can be said that a state's primary goals are the following:

1. Acquiring production inputs at the lowest possible cost
2. Increasing the volume and variety of its production
3. Exploring new markets to sell its products
4. Ensuring national security in the process

These four simplified objectives encapsulate the essence of most state policies. Variations between countries primarily lie in their methods of implementing these goals. These objectives compel nations to establish new alliances, explore new sectors, and sometimes engage in military operations. To construct a comprehensive profile of a specific country, research questions derived from these four objectives are useful:

1. What are the key production resources for country X?
2. Which countries are the main trading partners of country X?

3. Which products are major exports for country X?
4. With which countries does country X aim to expand trade in the future?
5. What are the future production and export goals of country X?
6. What are the primary security threats to country X?
7. What strategies does country X have to address these security challenges?

Research Guiding Questions

Understanding a country's objectives provides crucial insights into how it might utilize cyber operations in the future. The expanded list of questions given here can guide our foundational research about a country. We will explore this concept further with an example in the following section.

Before moving on please check out the CIA World Factbook[4]. It will be a crucial resource for our research along with several others.

Category	Question
Geographic location	What is the geographic location of {{country}}?
	What are its geographical properties?
	Which countries surround the {{country}}?

---

4 https://www.cia.gov/the-world-factbook/countries/

Natural resources and trade routes	What natural resources are found in {{country}}, and where are they located?
	Are there significant trade routes, and if so, where do they pass through?
	Are there any pipelines for resources like gas, water, and electricity to other countries? If so, what are the routes of these pipelines?
Demographics and political structure	What is the ethnic and religious distribution of {{country}}?
	What is the political structure and governance regime?
	Who are the key figures, institutions, and authorities holding power in politics?
	Who are the opponents of the regime?
	Which countries support the opposition?
Economics	What is the economic structure of {{country}} (industry-based, consumption-based, etc.)?
	What are the major components of state revenue?
	What are the most important economic sectors?
	What are {{country}}'s biggest export and import products?

	Who are the major trading partners in exports and imports?
Military	What is the structure of {{country}}'s armed forces?
	What are its main military capabilities?
	Which capabilities does its security strategy rely on?
International relations	With which countries does {{country}} have military, economic, scientific, and diplomatic collaborations?
	Which countries provide support to {{country}}, and which countries does the {{country}} support?
	Who are its allies and rivals?
Relations with major powers	What are {{country}}'s relations with the USA, China, Russia, and its regional powers?
	What are its relations with neighboring states?
Threat perception and security policies	What is {{country}}'s national security concept?
	What are its national security priorities and medium-to-long term goals?
	How does {{country}} engage with countries or groups it is in conflict with?

	What are the greatest security threats the {{country}} perceives against itself?
	How does it utilize its armed forces and military capabilities?
Foreign policy	What is the foreign policy concept of {{country}}?
	What are the priorities and medium-to-long term goals in foreign policy?
	Which political instruments and alliances does the {{country}} use against rival states?
Economic policy and foreign trade	What is {{country}}'s economic policy?
	What are the priorities and medium-to-long term goals in foreign trade?
	With which countries does {{country}} plan to establish relationships to achieve its foreign trade objectives?

When exploring answers to these questions, one should remember that countries often vary their approaches based on the region or issue at hand. This variability can make it tricky to understand a country's international relationships. A key point to remember is that, ***outside of wartime, absolute alliances or enmities are rarely found.*** Take, for instance, Israel: despite its well-known alignment with the USA, it refrained from actively joining the sanctions against Russia over the Ukraine invasion, despite Russia's well-known alliance with Iran[5]. As another example, Turkey maintains its trade relations with Russia during the Russia-Ukraine war, while also providing significant arms support to Ukraine. These two examples highlight the complex nature of state-to-state relationships. As such, once you've gathered basic information about a country, narrowing your research to specific areas of interest will be more effective when exploring its bilateral relations.

Case Study : Iran

In this section, the fundamental details collected about Iran that is believed to influence its foreign policy will be summarized. These essential details are meant to aid in comprehending Iran's priorities and approaches within its foreign policy.

Key Insights

Iran holds a strategic geopolitical position with the world's second-largest oil and natural gas reserves and control over key sea trade routes. These resources and locations are critical in shaping Iran's foreign policy, especially in the realms of energy and maritime trade.

---

5 https://www.castellum.ai/insights/which-countries-are-taking-action-on-ukraine

1. Iran is working to expand its influence in neighboring countries by supporting proxy armed groups. It also aspires to enhance its geopolitical standing by developing nuclear capabilities. Consequently, Iran has been facing persistent economic and military sanctions by the international community.

2. A significant portion of Iran's export income is generated from oil and natural gas. The country is focused on increasing investments in these sectors, despite having a fragile, centrally planned economy. Efforts to diversify its economy are hindered by limited access to foreign investment and technology due to sanctions, and difficulties in integrating with the global market.

3. Iran's approach to Middle Eastern affairs largely revolves around religious and sectarian dynamics. Its major adversaries include the United States, Gulf nations, and Israel, while Russia, China, Syria, and various non-state armed groups are among its supporters. Its main regional objectives involve dominating the oil and gas market, controlling sea trade routes, and diminishing the influence of Sunni regimes.

4. Internal security in Iran is challenged by numerous groups opposing the mullah regime. Addressing these dissident groups is a high priority for maintaining domestic stability.

Based on these insights, we assess that Iran's medium to long-term objectives include:

1. Enhancing its diplomatic ties to boost international trade.
2. Securing technology transfers necessary for economic diversification.
3. Achieving status as a nuclear power.
4. Reducing the influence of Sunni regimes in the Middle East.
5. Gaining control over maritime trade routes.
6. Suppressing opposition to the ruling regime.

These objectives are likely to be the primary drivers of Iran's intelligence requirements, guiding their strategic focus and information gathering efforts in the coming years.

Basic Information About Iran

Iran, situated in Southwest Asia, is nestled between the Gulf of Oman, the Persian Gulf, and the Caspian Sea, sharing borders with Iraq, Turkey, and Pakistan. Known for its mountainous terrain, Iran ranks among the world's most mountain-ringed nations. These mountains surround several narrow basins and plateaus, the primary hubs for agriculture and habitation. Importantly, Iran controls the Strait of Hormuz, a crucial shipping route that's essential for the global oil trade, highlighting its significant influence on international trade routes.

Spanning 1,648,000 square kilometers, Iran's landscape is

predominantly mountainous, interspersed with lush green areas. The country's highest point is Mount Damavand, reaching 5,607 meters, while its lowest is at the Caspian Sea, at -28 meters below sea level.

Iran shares its land boundaries with several countries: Turkey, Azerbaijan, Armenia, Iraq, Pakistan, Afghanistan, and Turkmenistan.

Natural Resources

Iran is notably rich in natural resources, particularly oil and natural gas, which are the first to come to mind when thinking of the country. Its wealth in resources and strategic trade routes is largely attributed to its geographic location, with direct links to Gulf countries. This, coupled with increasing investments in sea-based trade logistics, significantly bolsters Iran's economy. A closer look at Iran's natural resources and trade routes includes:

Oil and Natural Gas: Iran boasts one of the world's largest oil reserves, with an estimated 208 billion barrels. The southern region of Iran is rich in oil and natural gas reserves, with more abundant underground resources, making it a prime area for energy companies' exploration and extraction efforts. Iran's southern coast lies along the Gulf of Oman and the Persian Gulf, making these areas pivotal for sea-route energy exports. Consequently, energy production and storage facilities are built close to these coastal regions.

Salt Basins: Southern Iran features significant salt basins, crucial for accumulating oil and natural gas, hence rendering drilling in these areas more fruitful.

Zinc and Copper: Iran is home to the world's largest zinc reserve and second-largest copper reserve, primarily located in the Kerman and Hormozgan regions.

Iron Ore: Ranking ninth globally in iron ore reserves, Iran's major extraction areas include Kerman, Hormozgan, and the Northeast.

Gold: Iran has gold reserves, estimated to be around 320 tons, based on geological surveys.

Agriculture

Rich in arable lands, especially around major cities such as Tehran, Mashhad, Isfahan, Tabriz, and Shiraz, about one-quarter of the Iranian population works in agriculture and livestock. These include grains like wheat, barley, corn, rice; sugar beet and cane; fruits like grapes and apples; citrus, dates, pistachios, cotton, and onions. There's growth in the production of potatoes, soybeans, rice, wheat, and some vegetables. Exported products include dates, pistachios, and various fruits and vegetables.

Per the Iranian Ministry of Agriculture, 80% of the country's food requirements are met through domestic production.

Economy

Iran operates a mixed economy largely steered by its public sector. With a GDP of $386 billion, a major share of this comes from private consumption, and about a quarter of the GDP is generated by exports. **Oil and natural gas are pivotal, constituting 82% of export income**, positioning Iran among the top global holders of these resources. Key trading partners include **China, UAE, India, and Turkey**. Iran is actively working to diversify its economy, which is currently heavily reliant on the oil and gas sectors. However, it faces significant challenges due to sanctions restricting Iran's access to international financing and transfer of technology. These restrictions also limit its global market access and economic growth, compounded by the vulnerabilities of its centrally-planned economic system.

International North–South Transport Corridor

The International North-South Transport Corridor (INSTC) is a significant 7,200 km cargo route linking India, Iran, Afghanistan, Azerbaijan, Russia, Central Asia, and Europe. This multimodal corridor includes sea, rail, and road transport.

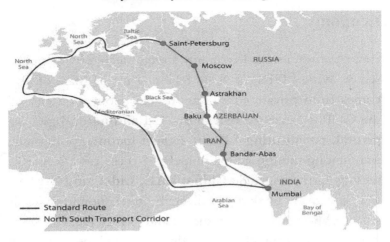

The INSTC holds substantial economic and strategic value for Iran for several reasons:

- The INSTC is vital in promoting Iran's economic expansion. It enhances Iran's trading capabilities with India, Central Asia, and Europe and propels economic growth through increased investments in Iranian ports and railways.
- Offering an alternative route to the Suez Canal, the INSTC becomes particularly significant in the context of the Ukraine War and sanctions against Russia. This alternative route boosts Iran's role in transit trading.
- The Chabahar Port, managed jointly by Iran and India, opens up Russian access to South Asia. The significant increase in Russian exports to India from April 2022 to February 2023 highlights this region's growing appeal as a new market for Russia.
- The INSTC enhances Iran's regional cooperation, especially with Azerbaijan. This collaboration stems from

Iran's efforts to seek external funding for its infrastructure and to leverage the corridor's potential. It also positions the South Caucasus as a key logistics center.

Military Involvements

Key Rivals: USA, Saudi Arabia, Israel, United Arab Emirates

Key Partners: Russia, China, Syria, Hezbollah (Lebanon), Hamas (Palestine), Shia Militias (Iraq), Houthi Rebels (Yemen)

Iran's national security concept is characterized by a few key principles: defending sovereignty and territorial integrity, preserving its Islamic revolutionary ideals, and maintaining regional influence. A significant aspect is deterring and responding to foreign threats, particularly from nations it perceives as adversaries. This strategy includes developing its military and defense capabilities, notably its missile program, and cultivating regional alliances. Iran also aims to enhance its strategic depth through proxy forces and unconventional warfare methods, while balancing its complex international relations amid ongoing sanctions and geopolitical tensions. For example, recent attacks by the Houthi on ships show how Tehran uses its proxies to project power and disrupt key shipping lanes.

Iran's military priorities in 2023 involve enhancing its capability to attack maritime targets beyond just the Persian Gulf and Red Sea, as indicated by its investment in "drone carriers" for its naval forces. These developments aim to amplify the threat to international shipping and maritime targets. Additionally, Iran's military activities show an increasing focus on using its Axis of Resistance, which includes supporting and coordinating with proxy forces in the region, to assert its influence and project power. This strategy includes a readiness to engage in attacks that disrupt regional stability and pose threats to international forces and interests.

Iran is involved in several military conflicts across the Middle East, each driven by its strategic interests in the region:

Syria: Iran actively supports the Syrian government led by Bashar al-Assad since the start of the Syrian Civil War in 2011. Iran's primary aim is to maintain a crucial ally in the region and prevent the collapse of the Assad regime, which serves as a conduit for Iranian influence in the Levant. Additionally, Iran seeks to counter the influence of Sunni-majority countries and militant groups in Syria. Economically, Iran is interested in securing access to strategic trade routes and markets in the Levant region, investing in Syria's infrastructure and reconstruction projects, and protecting its investments in Syria's energy sector, especially in oil and gas fields.

Yemen: Iran backs the Houthi rebels in Yemen, who have been fighting against the internationally recognized government since 2014. Iran's interests in Yemen are mainly related to its geopolitical rivalry with Saudi Arabia. By supporting the Houthi rebels, Iran aims to challenge Saudi Arabia's influence in the region and gain leverage over key maritime trade routes, such as the Bab el-Mandeb strait. Controlling or influencing Yemen could also grant Iran access to potential energy resources in the region.

Iraq: Iran holds significant influence in Iraq, particularly among Shia militias and political groups. Its interests include countering the presence of ISIS, preventing the emergence of a hostile Sunni government, and ensuring Iraq remains aligned with Iran. Economically, Iran seeks to maintain economic ties with Iraq, particularly in the energy sector, benefit from Iraq's stability and security for trade and investment opportunities, and use its influence in Iraq to bypass international sanctions and access global markets through Iraqi trade routes.

Lebanon: Iran supports Hezbollah, a militant group based in Lebanon with close ties to Tehran. Hezbollah acts as a proxy for Iran in the region, confronting Israel, countering Sunni extremism, and exerting influence over Lebanese politics. Iran's economic interests in Lebanon are primarily linked to its support for Hezbollah, which controls significant economic assets and institutions in Lebanon. Iran benefits from Hezbollah's control over smuggling routes and illicit trade activities, indirectly benefiting Iran. Additionally, Iran aims to expand its economic influence in Lebanon through investments in infrastructure and reconstruction projects.

Palestine: Iran provides support to Palestinian militant groups like Hamas and Islamic Jihad to challenge

Israel's dominance in the region and undermine Western influence. Iran's interests in Palestine are driven by ideological and geopolitical objectives rather than direct economic benefits. Iran provides financial and military support to challenge Israel's dominance and advance its revolutionary agenda. However, Iran's support for Palestinian groups also aims to enhance its influence among Arab and Muslim populations, indirectly benefiting its economic interests in the region.

Further Readings:

1. https://www.cia.gov/the-world-factbook/countries/iran/
2. https://www.worldbank.org/en/country/iran/publication/iran-economic-monitor
3. https://www.understandingwar.org/backgrounder/iran-update-may-19-2023
4. https://www.hoover.org/research/challenge-iran-2023
5. https://en.wikipedia.org/wiki/Axis_of_Resistance
6. https://www.cfr.org/global-conflict-tracker/conflict/confrontation-between-united-states-and-iran
7. https://en.wikipedia.org/wiki/Iranian_intervention_in_the_Syrian_civil_war
8. https://ctc.westpoint.edu/irans-unwavering-support-to-assads-syria/
9. https://iranprimer.usip.org/
10. https://www.bbc.com/news/world-middle-east-67614911

Could You Be a Target of Nation-State APTs?

As discussed earlier, whether an organization becomes a target of a cyber espionage operation largely hinges on its assets and how much they overlap with the interests of foreign countries' foreign policies. An organization could be targeted because of a product or service they offer, their connections with customers or suppliers, or because of high-profile individuals in the organization. Even the access an organization has to other networks or its large user base could put them at risk. To gauge the risk level, organizations need to ask themselves some key questions. The following questions are designed to help us do that. If you answer **Yes** to several of these, it may indicate you are potential targets for espionage.

An example will be used to broaden the topic. In the meantime, take a look at the questions below and consider how they apply to your organization.

Category	Risk Scale
Political Intelligence	1. Does my organization contribute to the policy-making of our home country? 2. Is my organization involved in activities related to our country's foreign policy? 3. Does my organization have individuals influential in policy-making within our organization? 4. Do any of the companies my organization is in business with meet any of the above conditions?
Economic Intelligence	1. Does my organization engage in significant export activities? 2. Does my organization conduct business activities outside our home country? 3. Does my organization possess intellectual properties that provide a significant commercial advantage? 4. Is my organization a publicly traded company with a high volume of trade? 5. Does my organization provide products or services to governments of other countries? 6. Do any of the companies my organization is in business with meet any of the above conditions?

Communications Intelligence	1.Is my organization a provider of communication products or infrastructure? 2.Does my organization have government agencies among our clients? 3.Do any of the companies my organization is in business with meet any of the above conditions?
Financial Intelligence	1.Is my organization a provider of financial transaction products or infrastructure? 2.Do any of the companies my organization is in business with meet any of the above conditions?
Geospatial Intelligence	1.Does my organization's product or service collect location data from users? 2.Does my organization process geographic or imagery data? 3.Do any of the companies my organization is in business with meet any of the above conditions?
Technical Intelligence	1.Does my organization conduct research and development in science and technology? 2.Is my organization's research and development directed towards an active market? 3.Does my organization's research and development topic have military applications? 4.Are there other countries investing in the same field as my organization? 5.Do any of the companies my organization is in business with meet any of the above conditions?

Military Intelligence	1. Does my organization develop or contribute to the development of products, systems, or services for military use?
	2. Is my organization a provider of widely used communication infrastructure?
	3. Does my organization own patents or intellectual properties that could be used for military purposes?
	4. Does my organization conduct technological research that could be used for military purposes?
	5. Do any of the companies my organization is in business with meet any of the above conditions?

Case Study: Solarix Dynamics

Disclaimer: The following example, designed to demonstrate intelligence planning, is purely fictional.

Located in the United Arab Emirates, Solarix Dynamics is a global leader in renewable energy and sustainability. With its ambitious projects, it plays a pivotal role in advancing the UAE's Net Zero by 2050 strategy. Here's an overview of Solarix Dynamics' activities:

- Solarix Dynamics, in 2022, significantly boosted its clean energy capacity by 33% to 20 GW and displaced 10 million tonnes of CO_2, emphasizing its key role in the global energy transition.

- The company has a global presence, with projects in over 40 countries, showing its potential in exporting renewable energy technology. Its ventures include utility-scale power plants and community grid projects, with investments totaling over $30 billion.

Impact of Renewable Energy on Global Power Dynamics

The advancement of renewable energy is not just an environmental or economic issue; it has implications for global politics, economics, and social development. Advancements in renewable energy are reshaping global power dynamics in certain ways. Firstly, the growth of renewables reduces the leverage of countries that have historically relied on fossil fuel exports for economic and political influence. As countries expand their renewable energy capacities, there's a decrease in dependence on fossil fuels. As a major exporter of both oil and natural gas, Russia's economy and its geopolitical influence are closely tied to the global demand for fossil fuels. Economies of countries like Saudi Arabia, Iraq, Iran, and the United Arab Emirates are also heavily reliant on oil exports.

Secondly, by investing in renewable energy, countries can achieve greater energy independence, enhancing national security. This is especially relevant for countries that rely heavily on energy imports. Many countries in Europe, like Germany and Italy, rely heavily on imported fossil fuels, especially natural gas from Russia. Japan and South Korea as well are major importers of fossil fuels due to limited domestic energy resources. Lastly, as one of the world's largest importers of oil and coal, India's growing investment in renewable energy sources is aimed at reducing dependence on energy imports and securing its energy future.

Given this background, it's reasonable to assume that Solarix Dynamics could be a target of espionage efforts from various countries. Let's explore the potential scenarios:

Major Oil Exporting Countries: Nations like Russia and Saudi Arabia might target Solarix Dynamics to gain insights into renewable energy trends that could challenge their oil-based economies.

Competitors in Renewable Energy: The USA and China, both vying for leadership in renewable energy, might be interested in Solarix Dynamics' innovative technologies and strategies for sustainable energy.

Regional Powers: Iran, given its regional interests and tensions with the UAE, might keep a close watch on Solarix Dynamics' projects, considering the potential shift in energy dynamics in the Middle East.

Emerging Economies Seeking Sustainable Energy Models: Developing countries with significant solar and wind energy potential such as India, might be interested in Solarix Dynamics' model to replicate its success in renewable energy projects.

It is evident that Solarix Dynamics must consider a range of threats during its cyber defense planning. Understanding the broader context of global renewable energy dynamics and regional geopolitical tensions will help in identifying the potential actors.

Final step of risk assessment is to identify threat groups operating on behalf of each identified country and mapping it all together. The following sources can be utilized in this regard:

1. MITRE ATT&CK Groups[6]
2. Mandiant APT Groups[7]
3. APT Groups and Operations[8]
4. ORKL.eu[9]

This exercise is primarily aimed at identifying the gaps in our collection capabilities. However, it's not necessary to individually list each and every country or APT group that might target us. The key focus should be on understanding which potential intelligence requirements could make us a target.

---

[6] https://attack.mitre.org/groups/

[7] https://www.mandiant.com/resources/insights/apt-groups

[8] https://docs.google.com/spreadsheets/d/
1H9_xaxQHpWaa4O_Son4Gx0YOIzlcBWMsdvePFX68EKU/
edit#gid=1864660085

[9] https://orkl.eu/

In this case, we observe that espionage targeting Solarix is driven by two primary needs:

1. Oil-exporting nations, potentially threatened by a renewable energy revolution, are keen to keep track of these emerging technologies and their market dynamics (Political and Economic Intelligence).
2. Countries aspiring to compete in the renewable energy sector are motivated to enhance their technical understanding of this technology (Technical Intelligence).

Collection Targeting Country	Reason	Known APT Groups
Economic-Intel Strategic RUSSIA	Oil exporting countries might target Solarix Dynamics to gain insights into renewable energy trends that could challenge their oil-based economies.	APT29, Sandworm, Energetic Bear
Economic-Intel Strategic SAUDI ARABIA	Oil exporting countries might target Solarix Dynamics to gain insights into renewable energy trends that could challenge their oil-based economies.	Unknown

Economic-Intel Strategic IRAN	Given its regional interests and tensions with the UAE, it might keep a close watch on Solarix Dynamics' projects, considering the potential shift in energy dynamics in the Middle East.	Cutting Kitten, Shamoon, Oilrig, CopyKittens, Flash Kitten, Fox Kitten, DEV-0343
Technical-Intel Strategic GERMANY	Countries that are aiming for the leadership in renewable energy, might be interested in Solarix Dynamics' innovative technologies and strategies for sustainable energy.	Unknown
Technical-Intel Strategic JAPAN	Countries that are aiming for the leadership in renewable energy, might be interested in Solarix Dynamics' innovative technologies and strategies for sustainable energy.	Unknown
Technical-Intel Strategic SOUTH KOREA	Countries that are aiming for the leadership in renewable energy, might be interested in Solarix Dynamics' innovative technologies and strategies for sustainable energy.	Darkhotel, Higaisa

Technical-Intel Strategic USA	Countries that are aiming for the leadership in renewable energy, might be interested in Solarix Dynamics' innovative technologies and strategies for sustainable energy.	Equation Group, Slingshot
Technical-Intel Strategic CHINA	Countries that are aiming for the leadership in renewable energy, might be interested in Solarix Dynamics' innovative technologies and strategies for sustainable energy.	Hurricane Panda, Night Dragon, Poisonous Panda, Violin Panda
Technical-Intel Strategic INDIA	Developing countries with significant solar and wind energy potential might be interested in Solarix Dynamics' model to replicate its success in renewable energy projects.	SideWinder, ModifiedElephant

---

Case Study: Tech Novelties

Disclaimer: The following example, designed to demonstrate intelligence planning, is purely fictional.

Located in Ukraine, TechNovelties is a firm that specializes in producing custom parts, catering to a wide range of clients in this area. It supplies a critical component for the UAVs of a Turkish defense industry client. Here is what is known about the relationship between these two companies:

1. The company TechNovelties, based in Ukraine, is responsible for producing an essential part for the Armed Unmanned Aerial Vehicles (UAVs) that are made by the Turkish firm SkyDefend Innovations.
2. A portion of these UAVs from SkyDefend is incorporated into the arsenal of the Turkish Armed Forces.
3. Additionally, some of these UAVs are exported to Pakistan, where they are added to the Pakistani armed forces' inventory.
4. Pakistan aims to use these UAVs to counterbalance certain military threats posed by China.

Given this information, it is reasonable to assume that the Ukrainian firm TechNovelties would be a target of espionage efforts from numerous countries.

Impact of Unmanned Air Vehicles on Military Affairs

In the context of cyber defense planning, the immediate inclination might be to investigate cyber espionage groups that focus on European technology companies. Yet, if we reverse our perspective and ponder which nations could be intrigued by the information held by TechNovelties, we gain a different insight. This requires us to reflect on the medium and long-term foreign policy, economic, and military goals of these countries.

From this perspective, several possible scenarios emerge (note that this is not meant to be a comprehensive list):

1. Given its hostile relations with Ukraine, Russia might be interested in TechNovelties, especially because it exports to defense industry companies, making it an attractive target for Russia.

2. SkyDefend Innovations, a customer of TechNovelties, produces UAVs that are slated to be part of the Turkish Armed Forces' (TSK) arsenal, presenting a potential threat to Turkey's neighboring nations. The capability of these Turkish UAVs to shift the balance of power in the Aegean Sea is a known source of concern for Greece. In pursuit of insights into Turkey's UAV production capabilities

and the quantity of UAVs in the TSK's arsenal, Greek intelligence might try to infiltrate TechNovelties to determine the annual volume of parts supplied to SkyDefend Innovations.

3. The effective use of UAVs manufactured by SkyDefend Innovations by the Azerbaijani military in the recent Nagorno-Karabakh conflict is well-documented. Consequently, Armenian intelligence could be interested in acquiring the technical specifications of the components made by TechNovelties, aiming to devise electronic warfare strategies to counter the UAV capabilities of Azerbaijan.

4. India, viewing the UAVs acquired by Pakistan as a potential threat, may consider infiltrating TechNovelties, paralleling Armenia's approach.

5. Targeting the Asian market, French companies are intent on selling their drones to Pakistan's armed forces. To support this aim, French intelligence might attempt to penetrate TechNovelties to further leverage this entry point into SkyDefend Innovations' systems, thereby uncovering the prices at which SkyDefend sells its UAVs to Pakistan.

6. For several years, Taiwan has been aspiring to develop UAV production capabilities. As a result, any entity (along with their suppliers) involved in manufacturing this technology would naturally be of interest to Taiwanese intelligence.

The type of threat landscape mentioned above is not actually something caused by the company itself, but rather a landscape arising from the customers to whom the company supplies its products. Therefore, every new customer, supplier, or market that a company enters introduces additional threats, influenced by the specific nature of its business activities. Without a thorough understanding of intelligence planning and utilization of geopolitical analysis, relying exclusively on region and industry for your research will fall significantly short in pinpointing threats relevant to your organization. An effective threat model should determine whether anything an organization possesses concerns the political, economic, scientific, and military objectives of other countries, and it should also catalog the potential risks that arise from such alignments or conflicts.

Final step of risk assessment is to identify threat groups operating on behalf of each identified country and mapping it all together. The following sources can be utilized in this regard:

1. MITRE ATT&CK Groups[10]
2. Mandiant APT Groups[11]
3. APT Groups and Operations[12]
4. ORKL.eu[13]

---

[10] https://attack.mitre.org/groups/

[11] https://www.mandiant.com/resources/insights/apt-groups

[12] https://docs.google.com/spreadsheets/d/1H9_xaxQHpWaa4O_Son4Gx0YOIzlcBWMsdvePFX68EKU/edit#gid=1864660085

[13] https://orkl.eu/

This exercise is primarily aimed at identifying the gaps in our collection capabilities. However, it's not necessary to individually list each and every country or APT group that might target us. The key focus should be on understanding which potential intelligence requirements could make us a target.

In this case, we observe that espionage targeting TechNovelties is driven by three primary needs:

1. In nations where UAV capabilities are posing a threat, there's a need to determine the number of UAVs held by a rival country and to understand the technical characteristics of these UAV components (Military Intelligence).
2. In nations striving for dominance in the UAV market, there is a necessity to obtain the trade secrets and intellectual property of competing UAV manufacturers (Economic Intelligence).
3. In nations aspiring to develop UAV manufacturing abilities, there is a demand for detailed knowledge about this technology (Scientific & Technical Intelligence)

Collection Targeting Country	Reason	Known APT Groups
Political-Intel Tactical RUSSIA	Given its active conflict with Ukraine, Russia might be interested in TechNovelties, especially because it exports to defense industry companies, making it an attractive target for Russia.	APT29, Sandworm
Military-Intel Strategic GREECE	The capability of these Turkish UAVs is a known source of concern for Greece. In pursuit of insights into Turkey's UAV production capabilities and the quantity of UAVs in the TSK's arsenal, Greek intelligence might try to infiltrate TechNovelties to determine the annual volume of parts supplied to SkyDefend Innovations.	Unknown
Military-Intel Strategic INDIA	India, viewing the UAVs acquired by Pakistan as a potential threat, may consider infiltrating TechNovelties, paralleling Armenia's approach.	SideWinder, ModifiedElephant

Military-Intel Tactical ARMENIA	The effective use of UAVs manufactured by SkyDefend Innovations by the Azerbaijani military in the recent Nagorno-Karabakh conflict is well-documented. Consequently, Armenian intelligence could be interested in acquiring the technical specifications of the components made by TechNovelties, aiming to devise electronic warfare strategies to counter the UAV capabilities of Azerbaijan.	Unknown
Economic-Intel Tactical FRANCE	Targeting the Asian market, French manufacturers are intent on selling their drones to Pakistan's armed forces. To support this aim, French intelligence might attempt to penetrate TechNovelties to further leverage this entry point into SkyDefend Innovations' systems.	Unknown
Technical-Intel Strategic TAIWAN	For several years, Taiwan has been aspiring to develop UAV production capabilities. As a result, any entity (along with their suppliers) involved in manufacturing this technology would naturally be of interest to Taiwanese intelligence.	Unknown

Understanding Peacetime Relations Between States

It's essential to examine how countries interact with each other, not just when they are at war, but also during peaceful times. This helps us understand their strategies based on their interests, which can be either similar or conflicting. In this article, we divide countries into three basic categories based on how other countries approach their relations with them: large powers, regional powers, and small states. By understanding these interactions, we gain insight into the strategies nations employ, which are influenced by their varying interests, whether they are aligned or in conflict.

Large Powers

These are countries that, despite being far from a particular region, have a significant impact on it through their political, economic, or military influence. While globally there are typically two or three superpowers like the USA, China, and Russia, more large powers can appear on a regional level. These countries are considered large powers in specific regions not because their power matches that of global superpowers, but because they have a strong influence far from their own borders. For instance, France and the United Kingdom have significant roles in Africa and the Middle East and act as large powers in these areas, even though they aren't global superpowers. The key difference between them and regional powers is that they influence regions far from their geographical location.

Relation with Large Powers

Regional actors have to either align with a large power or try to balance their influence. This choice depends on their own interests, the stance of other regional players, and the global political climate. However, it's important to note that a country may change its approach over time based on shifts in global and regional power dynamics and its own needs.

For example, in its final years, the Ottoman Empire and early Republican Turkey were under the significant influence of European powers like England and France. After World War II, the USA emerged as a global power and began to influence Turkey economically, prompting Turkey to shift its focus from Europe to the USA for industrial development. From the 1960s until the fall of the Soviet Union, the Soviet threat led Turkey to align closely with the USA. In the 2000s, as Turkey completed its industrial transformation and boosted its industrial output [14], it needed more resources, leading to engagement in regional power dynamics and competition with other regional powers like Iran, Israel, and Gulf countries. This resulted in Turkey reverting to a balancing strategy with the superpowers.

As this simplified historical overview shows, a country's foreign policy stance (balancing, aligning, and then balancing again) and focus (from Europe to the USA to multipolar) can shift multiple times even within a century. These changes are driven by various factors such as economic changes, shifts in global power, evolving security needs, and the roles of other regional actors. Therefore, assessing countries based on their economic and security needs rather than their political and ideological statements provides a clearer understanding of their foreign policies. It's also vital to recognize that alliances and rivalries are not absolute; countries are never always in competition or alliance, sometimes even during wartime.

---

[14] https://www.statista.com/statistics/255494/share-of-economic-sectors-in-the-gross-domestic-product-in-turkey/

Regional Powers

When countries in a region have enough economic and military power, they start to take a more active role in that region to meet their economic and security needs. Essentially, they use their political, military, and economic policies to sway events in neighboring countries in their favor.

Whether they're actually regional powers or not, all states try to influence their surroundings as much as they can through diplomacy (also known as 'soft power') or sometimes even covert operations. However, regional powers can change things more significantly because they have a lot more 'hard power'. This means that other countries in the region need to carefully manage their relationships with these regional powers. For example, Syria knows it can't achieve economic growth without the support of one or more regional powers, even though it aligns with a large power like Russia.

Regional powers differ from large powers in that they control key resources or trade routes in their areas. So, most economic activities in a region are actually more under the control of regional powers than large powers or superpowers. This is why smaller states, even if they align with superpowers, can't completely cut off their ties with regional powers. Superpowers themselves need to negotiate with regional powers on certain issues if they want to have influence in the region.

Regional Power <-> Regional Power Relations

Despite the fast pace of the digital revolution, industrial production is still crucial for economic growth today. This means regional powers are usually countries with advanced industries or those that are sitting on significant energy resources. Industry and energy go hand in hand; an increase in industrial output leads to a higher demand for energy, which in turn can boost industrial growth even further. Once an industry grows beyond a certain point, there's a greater need for external markets. Generally, regional powers are naturally competitive with other regional powers that have similar goals. Notably, this dynamic is very similar to the competition seen in 19th-century imperialist states, which eventually led to World War I.

It's fair to say that regional powers are mostly competitive with each other. However, they also depend on each other to be effective in the region, which naturally limits their competition. Sometimes, shared security concerns might push them to cooperate on certain issues. A good example of this cooperation is the Trident alliance [15], an intelligence-sharing agreement between Iran, Israel, and Turkey from 1959 to 1979. Although Iran left the alliance after the Islamic Revolution, Turkey and Israel continued to share

---

[15] https://www.foreignaffairs.com/articles/turkey/2015-05-07/tridents-forgotten-legacy

intelligence for many years. Relationships in this context are more complex and multi-dimensional than those with large powers, but the common theme is competition.

Regional Power <-> Large Power Relations

As discussed earlier, large powers are those countries that exert military, economic, and political influence far from their home regions to pursue their interests. Every large power must build at least a basic relationship with a regional power to effectively influence a region. Their presence isn't as permanent as regional powers, and maintaining a long-term military presence in a region can be expensive and unsustainable, as shown by the US's recent withdrawals from Iraq and Afghanistan. Therefore, the effectiveness of large powers increases as they strengthen their relationships with regional powers. Likewise, regional powers can enhance their control over their regions by fostering stronger ties with large powers. However, these relationships are dynamic, and the degree of alignment between the interests of large powers and regional powers determines the strength of their alliances. For instance, the US maintains strong alliances with Israel for security in Middle Eastern sea trade routes and with several Gulf countries for energy security.

Regional Power <-> Small State Relations

As previously mentioned, small states need to develop relationships with regional powers for their economic growth (like infrastructure investments and trade) and for security. In these relationships, regional powers seek to expand their influence through the small states around them based on their own needs. For example, Libya has allowed Turkey to explore for oil and gas within its waters in exchange for Turkish investments in energy infrastructure and economic support[16]. Furthermore, following Libya's civil war, Turkey has supported the Libyan National Unity Government, recognized by the UN, maintaining a military presence in Libya since 2020 [17].

Small States

Small states often find themselves in a complex web of relationships with both regional and superpowers. Unlike their more powerful counterparts, small states typically do not have the economic or military clout to exert significant influence on a regional or global scale. Instead, they must carefully manage their diplomatic ties to balance their own development needs with the strategic interests of more dominant countries. Navigating these relationships is not without its challenges.

Small states are often susceptible to pressure from more powerful nations and may find it difficult to maintain a

---

[16] https://libyaupdate.com/turkey-offers-contribution-to-libyas-energy-infrastructure-and-electricity-transmission-projects/

[17] https://www.france24.com/en/live-news/20221003-turkey-and-libya-sign-maritime-hydrocarbons-deal-1

consistent foreign policy that satisfies both their domestic audience and their international partners. Furthermore, their economic dependence on larger states can lead to compromises in policy-making and a loss of autonomy.

In the Middle East region, Qatar is an illustrative example of how smaller countries manage their complex relationships with more powerful neighbors and global superpowers. Qatar has used its considerable natural gas wealth to carve out a significant role on the international stage, far beyond what might be expected from a state of its size. Qatar hosts the Al Udeid Air Base, which is one of the largest US military bases in the Middle East, underscoring its strategic alliance with the United States. Simultaneously, it has managed to maintain good relations with Iran and Turkey, balancing its international relationships adeptly. Moreover, Qatar has invested in global real estate, sports, and media, using its wealth to generate soft power and secure a kind of cultural and economic influence that also serves its national security interests.

Conclusion

This exploration of peacetime relationships between states reveals a complex web of interactions driven by a mixture of competition, cooperation, and strategic diplomacy. From large powers influencing global politics to regional powers shaping their neighborhoods, and small states navigating their paths between larger powers, each plays a unique role in the geopolitical landscape. In the previous sections, we have examined how states employ cyber capabilities to fulfill their intelligence needs, reflecting their pursuit for economic, political and military policies. In the upcoming sections, we will delve into how states employ cyber operations during times of conflict, further unpacking the role of cyber strategies in escalating international tensions. The dynamics discussed here highlight the fluid nature of international relations, where alliances can shift and strategies can be redefined in response to changing global and regional circumstances. Recognizing the nuances in these relationships and the strategic use of cyber capabilities allows us to better understand the underlying motives and potential outcomes of state behaviors, which is essential for predicting future trends in global politics. This comprehensive approach to examining state interactions during peace provides a foundational understanding that is crucial for both policymakers and scholars in the field of international relations.

Wartime Cyber Operations

This section aims to offer a comprehensive analysis of cyber operations strategies, focusing on the typical targets and tactics employed by states during conflicts, drawing from historical observations. By studying these elements, we are going to have valuable insights for more accurate threat modeling, risk assessment, and forecasting in the realm of international cyber conflict.

Before we begin, I strongly encourage everyone to view Lincoln Kaffenberger's talk at the SANS CTI Summit [18]. This presentation lays out a solid framework for analyzing geopolitical cyber risks and offers some practical insights.

---

[18] https://www.youtube.com/watch?v=NJT0Y0Pj7e0

Wartime Activities Overview

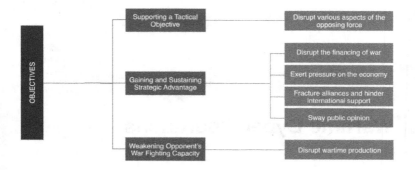

Ideally, the actions undertaken during or before a military operation should support at least one of these three purposes: 1. Achieving a tactical objective, 2. Gaining and sustaining a strategic advantage, and 3. Weakening the opponent's war fighting capacity. Let's explore a few examples:

Supporting a Tactical Objective: These activities aim to disrupt various aspects of the opposing force, enabling free movement of friendly forces during an operation. They are primarily tactical and are therefore carried out in coordination with the military operation aimed at achieving the specific objective. Such activities may include kinetic attacks targeting logistics, command and control systems, ammunition, and other supplies.

There is an increasing trend in militaries utilizing cyber attacks for similar purposes. Particularly, disruptive cyber attacks against information systems have proven to be highly effective. Some very recent examples are:

1. U.S. conducting cyberattack on suspected Iranian spy ship to inhibit the ship's ability to share intelligence with Houthi militants in Yemen. [19]
2. DDoS attacks at websites that provide critical information and alerts to civilians on rocket attacks twelve minutes after the Hamas attack on Israel.[20]
3. During Russia's full-scale invasion of Ukraine, cyberattacks were synchronized with missile strikes on critical infrastructure, including energy grids.[21]

In both of these cases, the attacks were coordinated with a kinetic military operation, and intended to disrupt some aspects of the opposing force.

Gaining and Sustaining Strategic Advantage: The purpose of these actions is to indirectly affect the warfighting capabilities of the adversary, often by weakening their Centers of Gravity (COG). COGs are essentially the key strengths that enable a nation to maintain

---

[19] https://www.reuters.com/world/us-conducted-cyberattack-suspected-iranian-spy-ship-nbc-news-2024-02-15/

[20] https://blog.cloudflare.com/cyber-attacks-in-the-israel-hamas-war

[21] https://www.csis.org/analysis/responding-russian-attacks-ukraines-power-sector

its war efforts. It's common for nations to focus on undermining their enemy's COGs during a conflict.

Potential COGs include:

1. Advanced intelligence and situational awareness
2. Superior mobility of military forces
3. The quantity and/or quality of arms and personnel
4. Funding for the war effort
5. Domestic public support for the war
6. Alliances and backing from the international community

The last three factors mentioned: funding, domestic, and international support for the war, play a significant role in influencing the war's outcome. Therefore, parties engaged in a conflict actively seek to disrupt the financing, exert pressure on the economy, fracture alliances, hinder international support, and sway the public opinion of the opposing state through all available means.

Disruptive cyber attacks targeting the key economic sectors of a rival state are often employed to exert economic strain. Additionally, these types of attacks can be used to apply diplomatic pressure on allies and neutral states, which will be outlined in the next sections. One thing to note is that a COG typically deteriorates over an extended period. Therefore, efforts targeting these are also likely to be sustained over the long term.

Weakening The Opponent's War Fighting Capacity: The purpose of these actions is to undermine the material capabilities of the opposing state's warfare. Cyber attacks aimed at disrupting key sectors such as manufacturing and energy can be seen in this light, depending on the targeted entity. For example, the aerospace, chemicals, automobiles, and parts organizations have all seen a significant rise in attacks.[22] These attacks often exploit the low tolerance for outages in the manufacturing sector, where IT service disruptions can halt production and lead to significant revenue losses. Another notable example of such activities includes the Stuxnet, Duqu, and Flame malware families. While these attacks were not conducted during wartime, their objective was to significantly hinder the nuclear capabilities of Iran and potentially the DPRK, targeting their nuclear warhead production infrastructure.

In the next section, we'll delve into the topic of hierarchy of targets.

---

[22] https://www.reliaquest.com/blog/cyber-threats-to-manufacturing-industry-1h-2023/

Hierarchy of Targets and Possible Course of Actions

As cyber defenders, our task is to realistically map out and prepare for various potential cyber threat scenarios that could arise in a conflict situation. This section is dedicated to outlining those scenarios, each defined by the nature of the potential target — opponent state, supportive states, or neutral states that might be drawn into the conflict. This process involves identifying the goals of potential adversaries (**objectives**), the conditions or events that could initiate their hostile actions (**triggers**), and the specific types of cyber operations they might employ at certain targets (**actions**).

Here's a breakdown of how this mapping works:

Opponent state: For an opponent state, we can expect actions like persistent cyber intrusions targeting the government, military, and intelligence agencies for critical intelligence, as well as disruptive attacks aimed at key industries and communication channels. These are maneuvers aimed at gaining a strategic advantage and crippling the warfighting abilities of the opponent.

Triggers: Armed conflict

- Objective: Gaining and sustaining strategic advantage
  - Persistent cyber intrusions targeting gov/mil/ intel agencies and their contractors, the defense industry, and think tanks for political, military and technological intelligence
  - Persistent disruptive attacks targeting key economic sectors to exert economic strain (e.g: energy, banking and finance, tourism, manufacturing, large private companies)
  - Persistent disruptive attacks targeting media outlets and communication systems to interrupt the flow of information
- Objective: Weakening of war fighting capacity
  - Persistent disruptive attacks targeting key industries to undermine the material production capability (e.g: chemicals, raw material, aerospace, energy, manufacturing and defense)
- Objective: Supporting a tactical objective
  - Coordinated disruptive attacks targeting communication and information networks in support of an ongoing military operation.

States offering political, economic, or military support to the opponent: When considering states that provide support to the opponents of one party, we prepare for scenarios where these entities could face similar cyber intrusions and disruptive attacks. These are likely motivated by a desire to exert economic strain or to discourage their alignment with the opponent of that party.

Triggers: Providing political, economic, or military support to the opponent. Public statements or other signs of support to the opponent. Advocating or supporting hostile policies in favor of the opponent. (e.g: sanctions, embargo)

- Objective: Gaining and sustaining strategic advantage
  - Persistent cyber intrusions targeting gov/mil/ intel agencies, the defense industry, and think tanks for political, military and technological intelligence
  - Persistent disruptive attacks targeting primary industries to exert economic strain (e.g: energy, banking and finance, tourism, manufacturing, large private companies)
  - Persistent disruptive attacks targeting media outlets and communication systems to interrupt the flow of information
- Objective: Discourage alignment with the opposing state
  - Disruptive attacks targeting key economic sectors or critical infrastructure in retaliation against any perceived political, economic or military support for the opponent state
- Objective: Counteract the propaganda efforts of the opponent
  - Disruptive attacks targeting media outlets, large private companies, and prominent individuals that publicly support the opponent state to discourage public support.

Neutral states: Neutral states, often overlooked, can also be significant in the cyber conflict landscape. They could be subjected to cyber operations if they show any inclination towards supporting the opponent of either party. In these cases, the objective often shifts to gaining a strategic advantage or countering propaganda efforts.

Triggers: Providing political, economic, or military support to the opponent. Public statements or other signs of support to the opponent. Advocating or supporting hostile policies in favor of the opponent. (e.g: sanctions, embargo) Political alignment with the opponent. (e.g: by joining NATO)

- Objective: Gaining and sustaining strategic advantage
  - Cyber intrusions targeting gov/mil/intel agencies, the defense industry, and think tanks for political, military and technological intelligence
- Objective: Discourage alignment with the opposing state
  - Disruptive attacks targeting key economic sectors or critical infrastructure in retaliation against any perceived political, economic or military support for the opponent state
- Objective: Counteract the propaganda efforts of the opponent
  - Disruptive attacks targeting media outlets, large private companies, and prominent individuals that publicly support the opponent state to discourage public support.

Counterforce and Countervalue Targeting

In military strategy, two primary concepts are counterforce and countervalue targeting[23]. Counterforce refers to military strikes aimed at the enemy's military forces and facilities, including bases, missile silos, and command centers. The objective is to weaken the enemy's military capability, often seen in the form of preemptive or retaliatory attacks. Countervalue targeting, on the other hand, focuses on non-military targets that hold significant value to the enemy. These include cities, industrial centers, and critical infrastructure. The purpose of countervalue targeting is to undermine the enemy's morale and economic capacity, and it often results in high civilian casualties and widespread destruction.

Cyber attacks linked with a military conflict can be considered as either counterforce or countervalue, based on their targets and objectives. For example:

1. Attacks on critical infrastructure, such as power grids, water treatment facilities, and healthcare systems, mirror the countervalue approach. These attacks aim to disrupt the normal functioning of society, instill fear, and potentially cause widespread damage and chaos. The recent documentation of Sandworm (now

---

[23] https://en.wikipedia.org/wiki/Countervalue

named as APT44) activities are the most notable.[24]Instances like the ransomware attack on the Colonial Pipeline in 2021, which disrupted fuel and gas supply across the United States, also fall under this category. Similarly, an attack on JBS Foods, one of the world's largest meat processing companies, caused significant concern over a potential meat shortage[25].

2. Cyberattacks that target military networks, government databases, and defense systems align with the counterforce strategy. These attacks seek to weaken the military and strategic capabilities of a nation. For example, Chinese spies placed malware in a Dutch military network in 2023, although the impact was limited due to network isolation. Another instance is the cyberattack against the Royal Canadian Mounted Police's networks in February 2024, which, although didn't impact operations, raised significant concerns[26].

These examples clearly demonstrate the application of counterforce and countervalue strategies in the context of military cyber operations[27]. In the next sections, we'll put theory into practice over two example armed conflicts.

---

[24] https://cloud.google.com/blog/topics/threat-intelligence/apt44-unearthing-sandworm

[25] https://cyberexperts.com/cyber-attacks-on-critical-infrastructure/

[26] https://www.csis.org/programs/strategic-technologies-program/significant-cyber-incidents

[27] https://carnegieendowment.org/2024/02/05/russia-s-countervalue-cyber-approach-utility-or-futility-pub-91534

Case Study: Russo-Ukrainian War

The Russia-Ukraine war, a significant and ongoing conflict, began in 2014 with Russia's annexation of Crimea and escalated into a full-scale war. This conflict has drawn global attention, particularly due to the involvement and support of various international actors. On one side, Russia, seeking to exert its influence and control in the region, faces staunch resistance from Ukraine, a nation striving to defend its sovereignty and territorial integrity. Ukraine's efforts are bolstered by substantial support from Western nations, including NATO member countries and the European Union, who provide various forms of assistance ranging from economic sanctions against Russia to military aid for Ukraine.

The ongoing Russia-Ukraine conflict has brought digital confrontation as an extension of physical conflicts, mirroring the complexities and strategic objectives of the warring states. In the specific context of the Russia-Ukraine conflict, with Russia as the acting party, the following detailed cyber operations strategy can be outlined:

Opponent State (Ukraine)
- Objective: Gaining and Sustaining Strategic Advantage
  - Cyber intrusions into Ukrainian government, military, and intelligence networks, especially targeting communication channels and data repositories, to gather intelligence that could offer strategic advantages.
  - Disruptive cyber attacks on Ukraine's key economic sectors like energy, financial services, and manufacturing, aiming to weaken the national economy and disrupt daily life.
  - Systematic attacks on Ukrainian media outlets and internet service providers to control the narrative and disrupt the flow of accurate information within Ukraine.

- Objective: Weakening of War Fighting Capacity
  - Targeting of Ukrainian defense manufacturing, including plants producing arms and ammunition, through cyber sabotage to hinder Ukraine's military supply chain.
- Objective: Supporting a Tactical Objective
  - Coordinated cyber attacks on Ukrainian military communication networks during key ground offensives to impair coordination and response capabilities.

States Offering Support to Ukraine (e.g., NATO Countries, European Union)

- Objective: Gaining and Sustaining Strategic Advantage
  - Cyber espionage against governments and defense contractors in NATO and EU countries providing military aid to Ukraine, aiming to uncover future military plans and logistics.
  - Persistent cyber attacks on the energy and banking sectors of these supporting nations, particularly those that have imposed sanctions on Russia, to create economic repercussions.
  - Ongoing cyber operations against media and communication channels in these countries, aiming to disrupt pro-Ukraine propaganda and influence public opinion.

- Objective: Discouraging Alignment with Ukraine
  - Retaliatory cyber attacks targeting critical infrastructure in countries that have provided significant military support to Ukraine.
- Objective: Counteracting Propaganda Efforts of Ukraine
  - Cyber operations aimed at media outlets and prominent social figures in supporting states, particularly those vocally opposing Russian actions, to undermine public and international support for Ukraine.

Neutral States (e.g., Countries Not Actively Involved in the Conflict)

- Objective: Gaining and Sustaining Strategic Advantage
  - Cyber intrusions into political and military intelligence networks of neutral states, especially those considering humanitarian or diplomatic support for Ukraine.
- Objective: Discouraging Alignment with Ukraine
  - Disruptive cyber attacks on neutral states' key economic sectors as a warning against siding with Ukraine or imposing sanctions on Russia.
- Objective: Counteracting Propaganda Efforts of Ukraine
  - Cyber campaigns targeting media and influential figures in neutral states to prevent the spread of pro-Ukraine sentiment and maintain a neutral or pro-Russia stance.

This strategic outline should be further refined with insights derived from the observation of the acting party's behaviors in past conflicts. The capability to conduct cyber operations does not guarantee their use in every scenario. States may choose to refrain from targeting critical infrastructure or key economic sectors due to potential political backlash or other considerations. Therefore, developing behavioral models based on historical patterns and tendencies of the involved parties is crucial. They can help in anticipating the moves of the adversary more accurately and in preparing more targeted and effective defensive strategies.

Conclusion

To conclude, the study of cyber operations during times of armed conflict presents a detailed understanding of the strategic objectives and methodologies employed by nations in the digital domain. This analysis is instrumental in enhancing threat modeling, risk analysis, and forecasting in the context of geopolitics. By identifying the hierarchy of targets and the diverse tactics used, from disrupting an adversary's economic stability to manipulating public perception, we gain critical insights into the evolving nature of digital warfare. This case study underscores the importance of envisioning potential future scenarios, especially during periods of tension and conflict. By doing so, we can assess their potential impact on our security, allowing for better preparedness and response. And the most critical lesson here is the need to integrate foresight into our cybersecurity practices.

Case Study: Nagorno-Karabakh Conflict

The Nagorno-Karabakh conflict, an enduring and intense territorial dispute between Armenia and Azerbaijan, escalated significantly in 2020. This complex conflict draws its roots from ethnic and historical claims, attracting attention due to the involvement of regional powers. Armenia, backed by Russia, and Azerbaijan, with support from Turkey and other regional allies, are engaged in a bitter struggle for control over the Nagorno-Karabakh region.

In the context of this conflict and from the POV of Armenia, the cyber operations strategy can be delineated as follows:

Opponent State (Azerbaijan)

- Objective: Gaining and Sustaining Strategic Advantage
  - Cyber intrusions into Azerbaijani government, military, and intelligence networks to gather intelligence for strategic advantages.
  - Disruptive cyber attacks on Azerbaijan's key economic sectors like energy and financial services, aiming to weaken the national economy.
- Objective: Weakening of War Fighting Capacity
  - Targeting Azerbaijani defense manufacturing, including plants producing arms, through cyber sabotage.
- Objective: Supporting a Tactical Objective
  - Coordinated cyber attacks on Azerbaijani military communication networks during key operations to disrupt coordination.

States Offering Support to Azerbaijan (e.g., Turkey)

- Objective: Gaining and Sustaining Strategic Advantage
  - Cyber espionage against Azerbaijani and Turkish governments and defense contractors to uncover military strategies.
  - Persistent cyber attacks on the critical infrastructures of these nations, particularly in response to direct military support for Azerbaijan.
- Objective: Discouraging Alignment with Azerbaijan
  - Retaliatory cyber attacks targeting critical infrastructure in countries providing significant military support to Azerbaijan.
- Objective: Counteracting Propaganda Efforts of Azerbaijan
  - Cyber operations aimed at media outlets in supporting states to undermine public and international support for Azerbaijan.

Neutral States

- Objective: Gaining and Sustaining Strategic Advantage
  - Cyber intrusions into political and military networks of neutral states, particularly those considering support for Azerbaijan.
- Objective: Discouraging Alignment with Azerbaijan
  - Disruptive cyber attacks on key economic sectors of neutral states as a warning against siding with Azerbaijan.

- Objective: Counteracting Propaganda Efforts of Azerbaijan
  - Cyber campaigns targeting media and influential figures in neutral states to maintain a neutral or pro-Armenia stance.

This strategic outline should be refined with insights from past conflicts. The capability for cyber operations does not guarantee their use in every scenario, as states may avoid targeting critical infrastructure due to potential political backlash. Thus, developing behavioral models based on historical patterns is crucial for anticipating adversary moves and preparing effective defense strategies.

Considerations

The Nagorno-Karabakh conflict, though marked by significant tension and military engagement, was relatively short-lived and regionally contained compared to full-scale global warfare. This context is crucial when assessing the likelihood and scope of cyber operations employed during the conflict. Given the conflict's short duration and limited geographical spread, it's less probable that extensive, strategic cyber operations were a primary focus. In such conflicts, the opportunity and necessity to develop and deploy comprehensive cyber strategies for long-term strategic advantages are often less compared to prolonged and widespread warfare.

Another critical factor to consider is the cyber capabilities of the warring states. In the case of Azerbaijan and

Armenia, neither has been widely recognized for possessing advanced cyber capabilities. This limitation suggests that the scale and sophistication of any cyber operations would likely be constrained.

However, this doesn't mean cyber operations were absent. In situations where the direct combatants might lack extensive cyber capabilities, two alternative sources often come into play:

1. **Allied State Support:** Cyber operations can be augmented through the assistance of allied states with more developed cyber capabilities. This collaboration can range from intelligence sharing to active involvement in cyber offensives or defenses.
2. **Hacktivist Groups:** The role of hacktivist groups, which operate semi-independently but in alignment with the interests of a warring state, can be notable. These groups often carry out cyber operations to express their support for a cause, leading to cyber skirmishes that mirror the physical conflict.

These considerations suggest that the scope and impact of cyber operations in the Nagorno-Karabakh conflict should be evaluated in light of these unique conditions. Each conflict presents its own set of circumstances, influencing the extent and nature of cyber warfare involved. Therefore, generalizing cyber warfare capabilities and strategies based on one conflict may not accurately represent the realities of another.

Documented Incidents

The Nagorno-Karabakh conflict actually featured distinct cyber operations that mirrored some of the support objectives in our threat model:

1. **Pegasus Spyware Attacks:** The Pegasus spyware was used extensively to target Armenian public figures, including journalists, human rights defenders, and officials. These attacks, occurring amid the conflict from October 2020 to December 2022, were significant in that they marked the first documented evidence of spyware usage in an international war context. The timing and the choice of victims strongly suggested these intrusions were part of active warfare, potentially on behalf of Azerbaijan. The Pegasus Project even revealed over 1,000 Azerbaijani numbers selected for targeting by a Pegasus customer [28] [29].

2. **Hacktivist Activity:** Armenian hackers targeted the website of Azerbaijan's public television station, while Azerbaijani hackers responded by attacking various Armenian websites [30] [31].

---

[28] https://www.politico.eu/article/warring-parties-spyware-azerbaijan-armenia-conflict-pegasus-hacking/

[29] https://www.amnesty.org/en/latest/news/2023/05/armenia-azerbaijan-pegasus-spyware-targeted-armenian-public-figures-amid-conflict/

[30] https://www.aljazeera.com/features/2020/10/11/nagorno-karabakh-conflict-ushering-in-new-age-of-warfare

[31] https://eurasianet.org/nagorno-karabakh-dispute-takes-to-cyber-space

Although our threat models may not fully materialize during a conflict, these documented incidents in the Nagorno-Karabakh conflict show that they still provide predictive value. We observed several scenarios that we had modeled, particularly intelligence collection and counter-propaganda efforts. The use of spyware for intelligence gathering and the exchange of cyberattacks between hacker groups for narrative control are examples that align with our threat model scenarios. These incidents underscore that even in a relatively short and regionally confined conflict, cyber operations can play a pivotal role. It's also a reminder that the unique conditions of each conflict, including the cyber capabilities of the warring states and the involvement of allied states or hacktivist groups, can shape the extent and nature of cyber warfare.

Conclusion

The study of cyber operations during the Nagorno-Karabakh conflict offers a window into the strategic objectives and methods nations employ in the digital realm. This analysis aids in enhancing threat modeling and risk analysis, particularly in geopolitical contexts. Identifying the target hierarchy and diverse tactics, from economic disruption to information manipulation, provides critical insights into the nature of digital warfare. This case underscores the importance of foresight in cybersecurity practices, preparing for potential scenarios that could impact security and developing appropriate responses.

Why States Go Into Armed Conflict?

States often enter into armed conflicts driven primarily by economic interests and national security concerns. Economic motivations can include the desire to control valuable resources such as oil, minerals, and strategic trade routes that are crucial for maintaining and enhancing a nation's economic strength and sustainability. For instance, access to oil-rich regions can significantly impact a country's energy security and economic stability, prompting state actions that might lead to conflicts. On the national security front, states might engage in armed conflict to neutralize perceived threats, extend their influence, or secure their borders against hostile neighbors. These security concerns are frequently intertwined with the goal of maintaining or altering the regional power balance to favor the state's own strategic interests.

Ultimately, while the triggers and manifestations of armed conflicts can be complex and multifaceted, the root often lies in securing economic gain and ensuring national safety, which are seen as vital components for a nation's survival and long-term prosperity.

Interstate Conflicts

Interstate conflicts involve disputes between two or more sovereign states, often characterized by military engagements and formal declarations of war. These conflicts can arise from a variety of issues, including political, economic, or security concerns.

Example: Russo-Ukrainian War

The Russia-Ukraine war is a very recent example of an interstate conflict. The conflict between Russia and Ukraine, particularly pronounced since Russia's annexation of Crimea in 2014 and the escalation in 2022, reflects deep-seated economic and security motivations. Economically, Ukraine's fertile lands and natural resources, including extensive deposits of coal and gas are of great interest. Additionally, Ukraine's strategic location as a transit route for energy supplies to Europe places it at the heart of regional energy security dynamics. From a security standpoint, Russia's actions have been motivated by the desire to secure its borders and maintain a sphere of influence in Eastern Europe, seen as critical to its national security. This is also seen as a response to Ukraine's closer ties with Western organizations like NATO and the European Union, which Russia perceives as a threat to its geopolitical standing.

Territorial Disputes

Territorial disputes occur when two or more states lay claim to a specific piece of land. Such disputes are often fuelled by the desire to control resources, strategic locations, or cultural and historical ties to the land. They can lead to military standoffs, economic sanctions, and prolonged diplomatic tensions. They often involve a complex mix of national pride, historical claims, and economic interests, making them particularly challenging to resolve. The South China Sea dispute is a contemporary example, involving several countries in Southeast Asia and China. These nations claim overlapping sovereignty over parts of the sea, which is a critical corridor for international maritime trade and is rich in natural resources.

Example: Nagorno-Karabakh Conflict

The Nagorno-Karabakh conflict is an illustrative example of territorial conflicts. This dispute involves Armenia and Azerbaijan over the Nagorno-Karabakh region, which, although internationally recognized as part of Azerbaijan, has a majority ethnic Armenian population. The conflict has deep historical roots but reignited into full-scale warfare during the late 1980s as the Soviet Union was dissolving, and again in 2020 with significant military engagements.

Economically, the region is strategically significant due to its location in the South Caucasus, serving as a corridor for pipelines transporting oil and gas from the Caspian Sea to global markets. Control over Nagorno-Karabakh would provide either country with strategic leverage over important energy routes, which are critical for regional economies. From a national security perspective, both Armenia and Azerbaijan view control over the region as vital to their national integrity and security. For Armenia, Nagorno-Karabakh is seen as a historic part of its homeland, deeply tied to Armenian identity and security. Azerbaijan, on the other hand, views the reclamation of the region as critical to restoring its territorial integrity and reducing perceived threats to its sovereignty.

Frozen Conflicts

A frozen conflict typically arises when active conflict ceases, yet the legal and political disputes that led to the conflict remain unaddressed[32]. These disputes often involve issues of sovereignty, self-determination, territorial control, and

---

[32] https://en.wikipedia.org/wiki/Frozen_conflict

ethnic division. The absence of a formal peace treaty or a definitive agreement leaves the involved parties in a limbo, unable to fully revert to a state of peace or revert to full-scale war. The situation is further complicated by the lack of recognized legal status for the conflicting parties, which impedes formal international negotiations and conflict resolution processes.

Frozen conflicts are significant because they not only represent unresolved historical issues but also often predict future conflicts. The persistent instability in these regions can lead to sporadic outbreaks of violence and may escalate into larger conflicts if provoked by internal developments or external influences. The uncertainty and ongoing grievances can exacerbate nationalistic sentiments, provoke militarization, and hinder economic and social development, creating cycles of tension and violence that may reignite at any point.

A defining characteristic of many frozen conflicts is the involvement of major powers, who may support different sides of the conflict through economic aid, military supplies, or political backing. This external support can perpetuate the conflict by providing the means to continue fighting and by complicating diplomatic efforts to resolve the issues at hand. Major powers often engage in these conflicts by proxy as part of broader geopolitical strategies, seeking to extend their influence or counteract the influence of rival powers in key regions.

Example: The Korean Peninsula

The situation on the Korean Peninsula is one of the most enduring examples of a frozen conflict. Following the Korean War (1950-1953), North and South Korea have remained technically at war, as the conflict was only halted by an armistice and not concluded with a peace treaty. The continued division of Korea is a result of ideological, political, and military tensions, underpinned by the significant involvement of major powers such as the United States and China.

North Korea's pursuit of nuclear capabilities and the regular military exercises by South Korea and the United States in the region exemplify how frozen conflicts can maintain high levels of military readiness and strategic maneuvering. The absence of a formal peace treaty perpetuates uncertainty and keeps the peninsula in a constant state of alertness, affecting regional security dynamics.

Tracking Global Conflicts

It's crucial for organizations to keep an eye on interstate, territorial, and even the frozen conflicts. These conflicts are often linked to a rise in cyber attacks from hacktivist groups or nation-states, which can pose significant security risks.

Sources like the Council on Foreign Relations[33] and the International Crisis Group[34] provide ongoing updates on active and frozen conflicts around the world.

Step 1: Use these conflict tracking tools to identify ongoing armed conflicts that might affect your organization based on where you operate. This helps you understand the specific geopolitical risks to your security.

Step 2: Analyze each conflict to determine your country's position—whether it's directly involved, supports one of the sides, or is neutral. This stance can greatly influence the type and amount of cyber attacks your organization may face.

Step 3: Apply the Hierarchy of Targets and Objectives - Triggers - Actions frameworks from earlier chapters to pinpoint what might trigger a cyber attack against your country or organization. Understanding these potential triggers helps you predict and prepare for security threats.

Step 4: Regularly monitor news sources and set up alerts for new geopolitical developments that could lead to an increase in cyber attacks. Staying proactive in this way allows your organization to adjust its security measures as needed, helping to reduce the impact of any cyber threats that arise due to armed conflicts.

---

[33] https://www.cfr.org/global-conflict-tracker

[34] https://www.crisisgroup.org/crisiswatch

By actively monitoring global conflicts and understanding their cybersecurity implications, organizations can better protect themselves against the complex risks posed by international disputes and conflicts. In the following chapter, we will apply this four-step methodology over an example.

Case Study: Ukrainian Hacktivists

In this chapter we will be focusing on a series of cyber attacks targeting Turkish airports, an event that's particularly interesting given Turkey's unique position in the ongoing conflict between Russia and Ukraine. We'll try to explore why these attacks happened, what Turkey's role in the larger Russia-Ukraine conflict might mean in this context, and how cyber tactics are becoming key tools in the arsenal of countries and groups looking to push their agendas on the world stage.

Lastly, we'll extract insights and make forecasts which we can use to preposition our defenses against potential changes in the geopolitical landscape. Through this analysis, we aim to show a practical example of how the frameworks from previous chapters can help monitor global conflicts and their effects on cyber risk.

The Incident

During the earlier stages of the Russia-Ukraine conflict, several Turkish airports were hit by intense DDoS attacks, thought to be carried out by Ukrainian hacktivists. During this attack, messages demanding the halt of flights to Russia were inserted into the HTTP packets, specifically stating "Stop flights to Russia" and "Cancel flights to Russia". Notably, Turkey is not directly involved in the conflict between Russia and Ukraine.

In response to these cyber attacks, the airports took action by blocking the HTTP requests that contained the word "Russia". Afterwards, the hackers did not adapt their attack against this measure. Also, no hacktivist group claimed responsibility for it afterwards.

Background and Turkey's Stance on the Conflict

Turkey holds significant geopolitical significance in the context of the Russia-Ukraine conflict due to several key factors:

1. Turkey controls the Bosporus and Dardanelles straits, which are vital maritime routes connecting the Black Sea to the Mediterranean. This control gives Turkey substantial influence over Russian naval access, especially for Russia's Black Sea Fleet based in Sevastopol, Crimea.

2. Despite being a NATO member, Turkey has pursued an independent foreign policy that often includes cooperation with Russia. This includes purchasing the Russian S-400 missile defense system, which caused friction with NATO allies. Turkey's ability to maintain relationships with both Western countries and Russia places it in a unique position to influence or mediate in the conflict.

3. Turkey has provided significant military support to Ukraine, most notably the Bayraktar TB2 drones, which have been effectively used by Ukrainian forces. This military assistance enhances Ukraine's defense capabilities against Russian aggression.

4. Turkey is a key transit country for Russian oil and gas pipelines to Europe, notably the TurkStream pipeline. This role in energy transit gives Turkey leverage in the region's energy dynamics, especially relevant given the conflict's impact on global energy markets.

5. Turkey has offered to mediate between Russia and Ukraine and has hosted diplomatic talks. Its unique position as a country with good relations with both Russia and Ukraine enhances its potential as a mediator.

6. Turkey has significant trade relations with both Russia and Ukraine, including in the agricultural and energy sectors. The conflict has implications for Turkey's trade dynamics, especially concerning grain and energy imports.

7. Turkey is a popular destination for Russian tourists, and the Russian market is important for Turkey's tourism industry. Economic ties between Turkey and Russia, including Russian investments in Turkey, add another layer to their complex relationship.

In summary, Turkey's geopolitical significance in the Russia-Ukraine conflict stems from its strategic geographic location, its role in regional energy dynamics, its military capabilities, and its unique position in balancing relations with NATO, Russia, and Ukraine. Turkey's actions and policies can significantly influence the conflict's dynamics and the broader regional security landscape.

Making Sense of the DDOS Incident

DDoS and other disruptive cyber attacks have increasingly become tools of "coercive diplomacy". In the past, various state and non-state actors have utilized these cyber tactics as a means to exert pressure, influence policy decisions, or retaliate against actions deemed contrary to their interests in a less confrontational way. One notable example is the 2007 cyber attacks on Estonia amid the country's disagreement with Russia about the relocation of the Bronze Soldier of Tallinn, an elaborate Soviet-era grave marker, as well as war graves in Tallinn[35]. In light of these precedents, let's assume that the attack on Turkish airports is also an attempt at using cyber capabilities for coercive diplomacy, and try to explore possible objectives behind it. Without clear attribution, Turkey may find it challenging to respond diplomatically. The uncertainty could lead to heightened tensions and suspicions, not just towards Ukraine but potentially towards other nations or independent cyber groups.

In this brainstorming scenario, analysts can employ frameworks such as STEMPLES or DIMEFIL, along with SAT like Outside-in thinking and 1–2–4, to envision various scenarios and gain a comprehensive understanding of the factors at play in any given situation. Subsequently, these scenarios can be organized into broader hypotheses, followed by the application of contrarian techniques to question each hypothesis. Analysis of Competing Hypotheses can then be utilized to pinpoint the most probable scenarios.

---

[35] https://www.cfr.org/cyber-operations/estonian-denial-service-incident

In our case, the majority of scenarios center around four possibilities, assuming that the hacktivist group is indeed acting in alignment with Ukraine's interests (which may not be the case):

Hypothesis 1 - Pressure on Neutrality

- **How:** Ukrainian hacktivists launch targeted DDoS attacks on Turkish civil aviation systems, causing flight delays, cancellations, and operational chaos. These attacks are aiming to disrupt but not completely destroy the infrastructure, indicating a desire for signaling rather than long-term harm.

- **Impact:** Such disruptions would draw significant public attention in Turkey, highlighting the Ukraine-Russia conflict's direct impact on Turkey. It puts pressure on the Turkish government to reconsider its neutral stance, as continued neutrality might mean enduring ongoing disruptions.

Hypothesis 2 - Economic Leverage

- **How:** By disrupting key economic sectors like civil aviation, Ukrainian hacktivists aim to cause a ripple effect in the Turkish economy. The travel industry, particularly tourism, which may include a substantial number of Russian tourists, is directly impacted.

- **Impact:** The economic strain could lead to public discontent in Turkey and force the government to reassess its economic relations and policies towards Russia, especially if the public or political voices draw a direct line between the disruption and Turkey's stance on the conflict.

Hypothesis 3 - Disrupt Russia-Turkey Connectivity

- **How:** Targeting transport and logistics infrastructure, specifically those used for Russia-Turkey connections, the hacktivists aim to disrupt the movement of goods, people, and potentially even diplomatic or military resources between the two nations.

- **Impact:** This disruption would inconvenience Russian businesses and travelers, potentially leading to financial losses. It may also hinder any covert or overt support Russia receives through Turkish channels.

Hypothesis 4 - Retaliatory Action

- **How:** This scenario implies a more aggressive stance from Ukrainian hacktivists. They target Turkish infrastructure as a direct response to what they perceive as Turkey's support or facilitation to Russia. The attacks might be more frequent or severe, aiming to send a clear message of disapproval.

- **Impact:** It serves as a public and global signal of Ukraine's disapproval of Turkey's actions or policies regarding Russia. This could mobilize public opinion in both countries and internationally, depending on the media coverage and public perception of the attacks.

Hypothesis 2 appears less convincing because the attack was deliberately designed to have minimal disruptive effects. Similarly, Hypothesis 4 is not strong, as there was no immediate need for Ukraine to retaliate when the incident occurred. Additionally, the DDoS attack was not modified to sustain its disruptive impact, and the absence of any hacktivist group claiming responsibility further undermines Hypothesis 4.

This analysis primarily supports **Hypotheses 1** and **3** as the most probable scenarios. Next, we will focus on translating these conclusions into forecasting models for enhancing cyber defense strategies.

Indications of Change: What actions in the future could trigger a similar disruptive cyber attack against Turkey?

While purely speculative, there are certain actions by Turkey that could hypothetically trigger a cyber-disruptive attack from either Russia or Ukraine, considering the complex dynamics of the Russia-Ukraine conflict. Here are some hypothetical scenarios:

Future scenarios: Turkey leaning in favor of Russia

Scenario A	
Military	If Turkey decides to stop supplying Bayraktar TB2 drones or other UAVs to Ukraine, a move that could significantly impact Ukraine's military capabilities, it might provoke a cyber response from Ukraine as a form of protest or to pressure a reversal of this decision.

Diplomatic	Should Turkey take steps such as recognizing territories annexed by Russia or openly opposing international sanctions against Russia, it would represent a significant shift in its diplomatic stance. Ukraine might view this as directly opposing its sovereignty and territorial integrity, potentially leading to Ukrainian cyber operations targeting Turkish diplomatic communications or platforms.
Economic	The grain export deal, brokered with the involvement of the United Nations and Turkey, allows Ukraine to export agricultural products through the Black Sea despite the ongoing conflict. Any move by Turkey to restrict or halt these exports could be perceived by Ukraine as economically hostile. In response, Ukraine might consider cyber operations aiming to disrupt operations and draw international attention to the issue.
Social	If the Turkish government were to enforce censorship against pro-Ukrainian media or civil society groups within Turkey, it could lead to Ukrainian cyber responses. These might aim at disrupting Turkish state media or government communication channels to protest against the suppression and highlight the issue intern

Future scenarios: Turkey leaning in favor of Ukraine

Scenario B	
Military	If Turkey significantly ramps up its military support to Ukraine, especially with advanced weaponry or intelligence that could decisively impact the battlefield, it might provoke a cyber response from Russia as a form of retaliation or to disrupt this support.
Military - II	Turkey controls the Bosphorus and Dardanelles straits, which are crucial for naval access from the Black Sea to the Mediterranean. If Turkey were to open up these straits to Western military ships, it could be perceived as a shift in its strategic stance, potentially favoring NATO interests. Such a move might be seen as a hostile act by Russia. This could potentially provoke a cyber response from Russia as a form of retaliation or to exert political pressure on Turkey.
Diplomatic	Any major diplomatic escalations, such as Turkey's recognition of certain territories or political entities in a way that is unfavorable to Russia, could lead to heightened tensions, potentially escalating to the cyber domain.
Economic	Should Turkey join or lead significant economic sanctions against Russia, particularly in critical sectors like energy, it could trigger a cyber retaliation aimed at disrupting Turkey's economic or financial sectors.

Social	Strong public statements or media campaigns by Turkish officials that are highly critical of Russia, especially if they gain international attention, could provoke cyber actions as a form of political signaling or to disrupt these information campaigns.

It's important to underline that these scenarios are speculative, formulated on the basis of historical patterns of cyber operations in international affairs. Nevertheless, devising these scenarios and monitoring substantial shifts in the geopolitical sphere can be immensely valuable for predictive defense. Armed with these insights, we can prepare for the most probable scenarios and their potential effects on our cyber security.

In a real-life application, it's beneficial to have a behavioral model for each country's cyber operations. This model would provide insights into the types of cyber operations a country might employ, the circumstances under which they would be used, and the potential targets. Such models can be developed by analyzing historical data of cyber operations during times of war or diplomatic tension. This approach greatly aids in accurately predicting the type and targets of potential cyber attacks in a given scenario.

To track the unfolding of these scenarios, we could establish Google Alerts using keywords tailored to each specific scenario, thereby initiating our monitoring process.

Google Alert Keywords for "Military":

- Scenario A: "Turkey UAV supply Ukraine", "Bayraktar TB2 Ukraine", "Turkey military support Ukraine"
- Scenario B: "Turkey military aid Ukraine", "Turkey intelligence support Ukraine"
- Scenario C: "Turkey Bosporus straits NATO", "Dardanelles straits military access", "Turkey Black Sea NATO"

Google Alert Keywords for "Diplomatic":

- Scenario A: "Turkey recognizes Russia annexed territories", "Turkey opposes sanctions Russia", "Turkey diplomatic shift Ukraine"
- Scenario B: "Turkey recognition political entities Russia", "Turkey Russia diplomatic escalation"

Google Alert Keywords for "Economic":

- Scenario A: "Turkey Ukraine grain export deal", "Black Sea grain export disruption", "Turkey Russia grain deal Ukraine"
- Scenario B: "Turkey economic sanctions Russia", "Turkey energy sector sanctions"

Setting up alerts in languages other than English can be useful, as the volume of news often increases nearer to its source, leading to faster updates. For our purposes, adding Russian, Ukrainian, and Turkish keywords tailored to specific scenarios would be good. Twitter serves as a valuable resource for rapid updates, although it usually requires more effort to filter through irrelevant information.

Conclusion

This case study highlights the importance of analyzing geopolitical tensions and alignments to anticipate and mitigate the risks of changing security landscape.

In conclusion, by dissecting such incidents, we gain valuable insights into the tactics and motivations driving cyber conflicts. This understanding is vital for developing more effective security measures and strategies in response to the complex interplay of technology, politics, and international relations.

Center of Gravity Analysis

The concept of a "center of gravity" (COG) in military strategy, first introduced by Carl von Clausewitz, refers to the source of power that provides moral or physical strength, freedom of action, or will to act. In military terms, COG are essentially the key strengths that enable a nation to maintain its war efforts. Centers of gravity vary between conflicts and adversaries, typically including:

1. Advanced intelligence and situational awareness
2. Superior mobility of military forces
3. The quantity and/or quality of arms and personnel
4. Funding for the war effort
5. Domestic public support for the war
6. Alliances and backing from the international community

It's common for nations to focus on undermining their enemy's COG during a conflict. Therefore, parties engaged in a conflict actively seek to disrupt the financing, exert pressure on the economy, fracture alliances, hinder international support, and sway the public opinion of the opposing state through all available means.

It has been noted that cyber operations also play a significant role in this context. One common wartime activity is information operations (IO) targeting the citizens of the opposing nation and its allies. This heightened level of IO activity requires an increased effort in intelligence collection for use in disinformation campaigns. As a result, a rise in cyber espionage activities is often seen prior to or at the onset of a conflict. In some cases, these are accompanied by disruptive cyber attacks aimed at exerting pressure on media outlets or prominent individuals who publicly support the rival state. All these efforts can be viewed as strategies to achieve and maintain information dominance.

I highly recommend checking out the following post from SecAlliance, which, in my view, excellently demonstrates the application of COG analysis in assessing potential cyber threats: Factors Influencing the Likelihood of a Systemically Significant Cyber Attack on Western European Financial Services[36].

---

[36] https://www.secalliance.com/blog/factors-influencing-the-likelihood-of-a-systemically-significant-cyber-attack-on-western-european-financial-services

Case Study: Potential Israel - Iran conflict

As the specter of conflict looms over the Middle East, we turn our focus to a potential military confrontation between Iran and Israel, sparked by the escalating tensions since the onset of the most recent Hamas-Israeli war.

This examination will seek to dissect the potential centers of gravity for each nation, pivotal elements that could be decisive in the event of a conflict. Delving further, we will explore how Iran has previously harnessed cyber operations as a tool of statecraft. Building on this understanding, our analysis will try to predict how Iran might deploy similar cyber tactics against Israel, aiming to weaken its adversary's centers of gravity.

Assessment of Centers of Gravity in a Potential Iran-Israel Conflict

In the case of Israel, critical centers of gravity include:

1. **Air Superiority and Advanced Technology:** Israel's qualitative military edge, including advanced aircraft, satellite imagery and missile defense systems like Iron Dome, provides it with the capability to preemptively strike and defend against attacks.
2. **U.S. Support:** Strong diplomatic and military support from the United States enhances Israel's strategic position globally.

Iran's centers of gravity, meanwhile, include:

1. **Ballistic Missile and Drone Arsenal:** Iran has developed a large arsenal of missiles and drones capable of striking distant targets, complicating preemptive strikes by its enemies.

2. **Economic Resilience and Control over Resources:** Despite sanctions, Iran has maintained economic stability through strategic partnerships, particularly with nations opposed to U.S. policies.

3. **Strategic Geographical Location:** Control over the Strait of Hormuz, a critical maritime choke point, provides Iran with significant leverage over global oil supplies.

Key Aspects of Iranian Cyber Operations

Iran's cyber strategy includes the employment of cyber attacks on a wide scale, ranging from disruptive countervalue attacks targeting critical infrastructure to sophisticated information operations aimed at breaking alliances and discouraging alignment with its opponents. Below are few examples:

Disruptive Attacks on Critical Infrastructure

Iran is historically known to engage in several notable cyberattacks targeting critical infrastructure. These disruptive attacks are part of a broader strategy to exert influence and respond to geopolitical tensions.

1. In 2019, Iranian cyber operations targeted Bahrain's Electricity and Water Authority, Aluminum Bahrain, and the national oil company Bapco. These attacks involved data destruction, significantly disrupting the operation of these critical infrastructure entities.

2. Similarly, Saudi Arabian targets have also detected disruptive activities from Iranian hackers, focusing on the destruction of vital data rather than espionage.

3. In recent years, Iran has executed various sophisticated cyberattacks against Israel. For instance, Iranian hackers attempted to increase chlorine levels in Israel's water supply in 2020, posing a significant risk to public health. Additionally, Iran targeted Israel's water system again, disrupting agricultural pumps[37].

Information Operations

Iran is known to utilize cyber influence operations heavily. These attacks often involve sophisticated social engineering tactics and misinformation campaigns designed to sow discord and manipulate public perception, both within its own region and globally.

1. Iran's information operations have been sophisticated and far-reaching. For instance, during the U.S. elections, Iranian hackers impersonated the extremist group Proud Boys to intimidate voters and spread disinformation. This operation involved downloading 100,000 voter records to send targeted, credible emails to Democrats while spreading false claims to Republican lawmakers and the media [38].

---

[37] https://www.timesofisrael.com/iran-cyberattack-on-israels-water-supply-could-have-sickened-hundreds-report/

[38] https://www.fdd.org/analysis/2022/10/28/the-dangers-of-irans-cyber-ambitions/

2. At the onset of the Israel-Hamas war, Iranian groups engaged in cyber operations that included spreading disinformation and re-using previously gathered materials. They claimed attacks on Israeli infrastructure like power plants, often exaggerating the impacts of these actions [39].

3. At another instance, Iran has deployed cyber operations that disrupted television programming in various countries, replacing content with propaganda to influence foreign audiences and promote its geopolitical agenda[40].

Discourage Alignment With Opponents

Iran also actively uses cyber attacks to discourage other states from supporting its opponents.

- During the Israel-Hamas conflict, Iranian cyber operations expanded their scope beyond Israel, targeting nations like Albania and Bahrain that were believed to be supporting Israeli efforts. This phase included more sophisticated influence operations and false claims of successful cyberattacks aimed at undermining the morale and security of the targeted nations[41].

---

[39] https://www.microsoft.com/en-us/security/business/security-insider/reports/iran-surges-cyber-enabled-influence-operations-in-support-of-hamas/

[40] https://blogs.microsoft.com/on-the-issues/2024/02/06/iran-accelerates-cyber-ops-against-israel/

[41] https://www.securityweek.com/iran-ramps-up-cyberattacks-on-israel-amid-hamas-conflict-microsoft/

Iran's Likely Objectives During a Potential Iran-Israel Conflict

Iran's strategic objectives in a potential conflict with Israel is likely to reflect a multifaceted approach. Based on the historical patterns of cyber attacks by Iran and Israel's assessed strengths, we can expect Iran to engage in extensive cyber operations aimed at disrupting Israel's command and control systems, targeting critical infrastructure to weaken the Israeli economy, and conducting heavy propaganda and information warfare to undermine international support for Israel prior to and during a military conflict.

- Objective: Disrupting Israel's Communication Systems
  - Cyber intrusions into Israeli government and military networks to gather intelligence and disrupt communications, aiming to hinder coordination and decision-making.
  - Targeted cyber attacks on critical infrastructure related to telecommunications and internet services to degrade Israel's ability to communicate effectively.

- Objective: Economic Warfare
  - Disruptive cyber attacks targeting key industries such as energy, finance, and transportation in Israel, with the goal of weakening the national economy and causing financial instability.

- Cyber sabotage of industrial facilities and critical infrastructure to disrupt production and supply chains, leading to economic disruption and resource shortages.

- Objective: Psychological Operations and Information Warfare
  - Heavy propaganda and information operations targeting both domestic and international audiences to undermine support for Israel and its allies, including the United States.
  - Utilization of social media manipulation, fake news dissemination, and cyber influence campaigns to sow discord, create confusion, and delegitimize Israeli actions in the eyes of the global community.
- Objective: Dissuading Support for Israel
  - Retaliatory cyber attacks against states providing significant military and diplomatic support to Israel, aiming to discourage further alignment and intervention.
  - Targeted cyber espionage and disruption of critical infrastructure in countries allied with Israel, particularly in response to direct military or intelligence cooperation.

Next Steps

In the above analysis, we've looked into the potential cyber activities Iran might undertake in a highly likely Iran-Israel conflict. Now, considering your country's stance in such a conflict, you can use these insights to create your own threat model. If your country's stance isn't predictable, it would be helpful to think about different future scenarios and track their emergence through a number of news sources. You can use tools like the Global Conflict Tracker or set up alerts with relevant keywords on Google Alerts as we mentioned in the previous sections. This approach allows us to anticipate the elevated risk of cyber attacks and inform our organizations proactively, giving us a lot more time for preparation, achieving a true proactive stance.

Analysis Process

So far, this book has explored how state policies are shaped by economic and security parameters, including how objectives are determined and how cyber intrusions are deployed to achieve them. Our goal was to illuminate the internal workings of states to enhance your understanding of state-sponsored threat actors. This insight allows you to adapt the analysis templates we've discussed to your own organizations and proactively assess potential risks from geopolitical developments.

However, possessing geopolitical knowledge alone does not guarantee accurate analysis. As frequently noted in the intelligence community, subconscious mechanisms significantly influence what we perceive as conscious thought processes. Personal experiences profoundly shape our mental worlds, and our thinking is also affected by biological limitations and evolutionary thought patterns.

Consequently, our perception of reality is inherently subjective, and the analyses influenced by these mechanisms often generate predictable thought patterns, sometimes leading to incorrect conclusions. These misleading patterns are known as cognitive biases.

An effective analysis process requires a deliberate effort to clearly display and scrutinize all assumptions and cause-and-effect relationships. To this end, Structured Analytic Techniques (SAT) are employed. These techniques are used in strategic intelligence analysis to help analysts think more objectively, systematically, and creatively, thereby aiding decision-making processes. They involve data collection, hypothesis testing, and evaluating different scenarios, particularly valuable in analyzing uncertain and complex situations to reduce subjective judgments and assess situations from multiple perspectives.

Structured Analytic Techniques are categorized into three groups:

Diagnostic Techniques: These assess the robustness of an analysis by reviewing the key assumptions and the quality of information. The primary aim is to challenge accepted assumptions and confirm the reliability of the informational base.

Contrarian Techniques: These methods challenge prevailing consensus or entrenched beliefs by bringing to light alternative scenarios and viewpoints that are often neglected. They prompt analysts to step outside established thought frameworks and consider events from varied angles.

Imaginative Techniques: Also known as creative techniques, these involve devising various future scenarios and establishing connections among them to thoroughly contemplate potential futures. They are particularly useful in situations fraught with uncertainties, allowing for the exploration of multiple alternatives.

Given the extensive literature on cognitive biases and structured analytic techniques, this book will not delve into these topics extensively. Numerous publications by the CIA, especially Richard J. Heuer's "Psychology of Intelligence Analysis," serve as foundational texts in this area.

This section aims to discuss techniques useful in geopolitical cyber risk analysis and explain their application in previous chapters.

We will cover the following techniques in this section:

- Key Assumptions Check
- Analysis of Competing Hypotheses
- Brainstorming
- Signposts of Change
- Contrarian Techniques

Key Assumptions Check

The Key Assumptions Check is a structured process designed to expose and scrutinize the basic assumptions underlying an analysis. Often, we unconsciously hold assumptions across various topics, which can turn out to be incorrect and lead to flawed conclusions. It's crucial to clearly state all relevant assumptions and evaluate the potential impact if these assumptions prove incorrect. We should identify assumptions that could significantly influence our analysis, determine what these assumptions hinge upon, and collect supportive and contrary evidence to reassess their validity.

Consider the example from the "Tracking Global Conflicts" section, where we analyzed the DDoS attacks on airports by Ukrainian hacktivists. This analysis was based on several key assumptions:

- Assumption 1: The individuals behind the attack were acting in alignment with Ukraine's interests.
- Assumption 2: The attack was driven by political objectives.
- Assumption 3: The attack deliberately targeted airline companies.
- Assumption 4: The attack did not aim to cause destructive effects.

The initial step involves documenting these assumptions and the rationale or evidence that led us to them. Next, by challenging each assumption's validity, we should explore alternative explanations for the observed phenomena. This approach ensures a comprehensive evaluation of all possibilities tied to our fundamental assumptions, aiding in steering the direction of our analysis.

Assumption	Assessment	Alternative Explanation(s)
The individuals behind the attack were acting in alignment with Ukraine's interests.	The message "CANCEL FLIGHTS TO RUSSIA" embedded inside the attack seems to be a call for action against Russia, suggesting that the attack was carried out by perpetrators supporting Ukraine.	1. The attack was actually a deception operation carried out by Russia or its allies, aimed at inciting hostility in target countries by portraying Ukraine as aggressive and harmful. This strategy also served to normalize Russia's own cyber attacks on the international scene. 2. The attack was actually an opportunistic attempt by hacktivists to gain popularity during the Russia-Ukraine war.

The attack was driven by political objectives.	The aforementioned message and the absence of any financial demands suggest that the motive is likely to be political.	1. The attack wasn't driven by political motives; rather, it served as a smokescreen to conceal a simultaneous data exfiltration effort. 2. The attack was actually an opportunistic attempt by hacktivists to gain popularity during the Russia-Ukraine war.
The attack deliberately targeted airline companies.	The alignment of the demand in the message with the target shows that airports and airline companies were deliberately selected as targets.	-

The attack did not aim to cause destructive effects.	The attackers made no attempt to circumvent the simple keyword-based blocking.	1. The attack aimed to inflict damage, yet the attackers did not have the technical expertise to bypass the security measure.
		2. The attackers chose not to focus on individual targets, as they were attacking multiple targets globally simultaneously.

In the second step, we need to evaluate each alternative explanation and determine how it could impact the results of the analysis or the actions to be taken. If an alternative scenario, when proven true, would significantly alter the course or outcome of the analysis, it requires special examination. In our next example, techniques like Analysis of Competing Hypotheses allow us to reach a conclusion by comparing alternative scenarios with the existing evidence.

Finally, create a list of key assumptions that are absolutely necessary for the accuracy of the analysis. Determine under which conditions or in light of which new information these assumptions might lose their validity.

Alternative Explanation(s)	Impact
The attack was actually a deception operation carried out by Russia or its allies, aimed at inciting hostility in target countries by portraying Ukraine as aggressive and harmful. This strategy also served to normalize Russia's own cyber attacks on the international scene.	If this scenario proves accurate, it could reshape the government's political response and necessitate changes to the predictive model.
The attack was actually an opportunistic attempt by hacktivists to gain popularity during the Russia-Ukraine war.	If this scenario proves accurate, then any political response would be ineffective, and the assumption of predictability would likely prove incorrect.
The attack wasn't driven by political motives; rather, it served as a smokescreen to conceal a simultaneous data exfiltration effort.	If this scenario proves accurate, any political response would be ineffective, and the direction of the investigation would need a complete overhaul.
The attack aimed to inflict damage, yet the attackers did not have the technical expertise to bypass the security measure.	This scenario does not affect the outcome of the analysis.
The attackers chose not to focus on individual targets, as they were attacking multiple targets globally simultaneously.	This scenario does not affect the outcome of the analysis.

In this scenario, keep in mind that our analysis aims to develop a behavior model capable of predicting similar attacks. Therefore, it's crucial that two key assumptions are correct for our analysis to be accurate:

1. The individuals behind the attack were acting in line with Ukraine's interests.
2. The attack was motivated by political objectives.

Analysis of Competing Hypotheses

Analysis of Competing Hypotheses (ACH) is a method used when multiple plausible explanations exist for a given situation. It involves comparing hypotheses with available data to refute as many as possible. The most supported hypothesis by the data is then considered the most likely scenario. The ACH process typically includes the following steps:

*   **Hypothesis Formation:** The process starts by identifying all possible hypotheses, ideally through brainstorming among a group of analysts with diverse perspectives.
*   **Evidence Gathering:** Analysts compile evidence and arguments, including assumptions and logical deductions, that support or refute each hypothesis.

- **Diagnostic Evaluation:** Using a matrix, analysts test each hypothesis against the available evidence, aiming to disprove as many as possible. They focus on one piece of evidence at a time and assess it against all potential hypotheses.

- **Refinement:** Analysts review the results, identify any gaps, and collect additional evidence needed to challenge as many of the remaining hypotheses as possible.

For instance, during the Key Assumptions Check, we observed that attributing the attack significantly influenced the direction of the analysis. Using the ACH technique, we determine which possibilities require further examination or at least identify what type of information is necessary to clarify the issue.

Hypothesis	E 1	E 2	E 3
The actor aligns with Ukrainian interests	1	0	0
The actor aligns with Russian interests	-1	0	0
Opportunistic / non-aligned actor	0	-1	-1

Evidence 1: The message "CANCEL FLIGHTS TO RUSSIA" embedded inside the attack seems to be a call for action against Russia.

Evidence 2: No hacktivist groups claimed responsibility for the attack, indicating that seeking fame or popularity was not the motive.

Evidence 3: The absence of any financial demands suggest that the motive is likely to be political.

If you recall, in the continuation of the same case analysis, we developed four hypotheses based on the assumption that Ukrainian hacktivists carried out the attack:

- Hypothesis 1 - Pressure on Neutrality
- Hypothesis 2 - Economic Leverage
- Hypothesis 3 - Disrupt Russia-Turkey Connectivity
- Hypothesis 4 - Retaliatory Action

After listing these hypotheses, our elimination of Hypotheses 2 and 4 was actually based on using the ACH technique.

We can clarify this process more clearly as follows:

Hypothesis	E 1	E 2	E 3	E 4
1. Ukraine pressures Turkey to maintain neutrality.	0	0	0	1
2. Ukraine seeks to disrupt the Turkish economy.	-1	0	-2	-2
3. Ukraine intends to disrupt Russia and Turkey connectivity.	-2	0	-1	2
4. Ukraine retaliates to Turkey's actions that favor Russia.	1	-1	-1	1

Evidence 1: The attackers made no attempt to circumvent the simple keyword-based blocking, indicating that the attack was designed to have minimal effect.

Evidence 2: There was no immediate need for Ukraine to retaliate when the incident occured.

Evidence 3: Turkey's neutral stance is crucial for Ukraine, having brokered a key grain export deal and provided significant military support involving the Bayraktar TB2 UAVs. Therefore, Ukraine will likely avoid actions that could damage relations with Turkey.

Evidence 4: There were no other (known) coordinated attacks on Turkey's key economic sectors.

As seen in the two examples, what is considered evidence is largely at the discretion of the analyst. Sometimes the absence of something, or the analyst's evaluations about the topic, can be included in the ACH as evidence. Therefore, every non-objective piece of data (such as interpretations or assessments) included in the ACH should be questioned separately, and the extent to which the hypotheses would be affected if this data proves incorrect should be assessed. If a significant piece of evidence relies on the analyst's interpretation, conducting a detailed investigation to disprove or verify this evidence would be beneficial.

Brainstorming

Brainstorming is a crucial process that enriches nearly every step of analysis. It is used to identify potential actors behind an attack, develop hypotheses to make sense of an event, predict an actor's next move, and generate alternative explanations for events. The more robust the brainstorming process, the more scenarios and possibilities are incorporated into the analysis, preventing oversight. Including people with diverse experiences and expertise in the process enhances the quality of brainstorming. Different perspectives help bring out previously unthought-of ideas and reduce the risk of group-think. Below are a few techniques that can be used for brainstorming.

Mind Mapping: Mind mapping is a technique that organizes thoughts around a main idea in a visual network. The main topic is placed at the center, and related sub-ideas branch out from it. This method is used to visually structure information and make complex ideas more comprehensible, enabling participants to easily see and establish new connections between ideas.

6-3-5 Method: In this method, 6 participants each generate 3 ideas, and the process is repeated 5 times. Participants begin by writing their ideas within a set time limit, then pass their papers to the next person, who expands on the previous ideas. This cyclical process generates a broad and diversified pool of ideas.

Round Robin Brainstorming: Round Robin ensures equal participation from all members. A question or topic is set, and each participant takes turns presenting an idea. Other participants remain silent until it is their turn to speak. This method ensures that everyone's ideas are expressed and that every voice within the group is heard.

1-2-4 Technique: This technique involves participants first thinking individually, then in pairs, and finally in groups of four. At each stage, ideas are examined and refined by more people, offering widespread participation and in-depth analysis opportunities.

Signposts of Change

The Signposts of Change technique is a structured analytic method used in areas like geopolitics or business to foresee significant future changes. This method involves creating indicators or "signposts" that show the development of a particular scenario, providing analysts and decision-makers with advance warnings before significant events occur. Analysts regularly review predefined indicators and monitor changes in these indicators to detect possible developments and trends. This technique facilitates strategic planning in uncertain and dynamic environments and supports decision-making processes, helping organizations to be better prepared for the future.

The analysis we conducted in the final part of the Ukrainian Hacktivist case is an example of this type of analysis. If you recall, after evaluating the case from Turkey's perspective, we developed hypotheses on what actions by Turkey might trigger another cyber attack in the future. We then identified key words related to the likelihood of these scenarios and began monitoring news sources. What we did here was a precise application of the Signposts of Change technique.

Scenario A: Turkey leaning in favor of Russia	
Military	If Turkey decides to stop supplying Bayraktar TB2 drones or other UAVs to Ukraine, a move that could significantly impact Ukraine's military capabilities, it might provoke a cyber response from Ukraine as a form of protest or to pressure a reversal of this decision.
Diplomatic	Should Turkey take steps such as recognizing territories annexed by Russia or openly opposing international sanctions against Russia, it would represent a significant shift in its diplomatic stance. Ukraine might view this as directly opposing its sovereignty and territorial integrity, potentially leading to Ukrainian cyber operations targeting Turkish diplomatic communications or platforms.
Economic	The grain export deal, brokered with the involvement of the United Nations and Turkey, allows Ukraine to export agricultural products through the Black Sea despite the ongoing conflict. Any move by Turkey to restrict or halt these exports could be perceived by Ukraine as economically hostile. In response, Ukraine might consider cyber operations aiming to disrupt operations and draw international attention to the issue.
Social	If the Turkish government were to enforce censorship against pro-Ukrainian media or civil society groups within Turkey, it could lead to Ukrainian cyber responses. These might aim at disrupting Turkish state media or government communication channels to protest against the suppression and highlight the issue intern.

Contrarian Techniques

Using contrarian techniques throughout the analysis process is crucial. Ideally, every assumption, evaluation, opinion, hypothesis, and even data considered objective should be questioned for its potential to be incorrect. While questioning every piece of information, especially using structured techniques, can be time-consuming, we often do not have the luxury to do so extensively. In such cases, it's vital to determine how the included information or emerging assumptions and hypotheses during the analysis change the outcome. Information and hypotheses that significantly affect the course of the analysis should undergo thorough questioning and research.

Contrarian techniques fundamentally involve assigning one or several members of the analysis team the task of defending a contrary viewpoint, similar to debate activities in high schools. The goal is not necessarily to reach a definitive conclusion but to critically expose the weaknesses in each hypothesis, creating a dynamic that encourages intellectual conflict.

Devil's Advocate: This technique is highly useful when one argument seems stronger than others, or when the team agrees on a single explanation. An analyst is asked to play the Devil's Advocate, investing all their efforts to propose an alternative explanation to the current consensus. This approach is used to enhance the objectivity of the analysis and to identify any potential weaknesses or biases. For instance, questioning our strongest hypothesis from the Ukrainian Hacktivist case ("Ukraine pressures Turkey to maintain neutrality") using the Devil's Advocate method could be beneficial.

Team A/B Analysis: This technique can be employed when multiple strong hypotheses have been formed, which makes reaching a judgment challenging. The process involves assigning different teams to defend each of the selected hypotheses and debating them. Each team prepares by researching in advance and considers what new information could refute the opposing team's hypothesis. Then, the opposing hypotheses are debated in a forum, and ultimately, a jury decides which defense is stronger.

We've discussed techniques that can enhance the analysis process in this chapter. However, the techniques developed in this field extend far beyond what is mentioned in this book. It's also worth noting that these techniques have faced criticism. Some, like the ACH, have been revised over time due to identified shortcomings and alternatives have been developed. Nevertheless, this book does not need to dwell on such details extensively. The main idea is to design an analysis process that includes all possibilities before reaching any judgment and deeply scrutinizes the hypotheses based on their impact on the outcomes. Such a well-designed analysis process, whether using Structured Analytic Techniques or not, significantly reduces the chances of incorrect judgments and ensures the production of high-quality outputs.

Further Readings

1. https://www.cia.gov/resources/csi/books-monographs/psychology-of-intelligence-analysis-2/

ABOUT THE AUTHOR

Robin Dimyanoglu is the Red Team Lead at HelloFresh Global, based in Berlin, Germany. With extensive experience in Cyber Threat Intelligence and Threat-Informed Defense, Robin is inspired to bring in concepts from war and intelligence studies into cyber security. His expertise spans offensive security, threat intelligence, and malware reverse engineering, refined over years of working in diverse and challenging environments.

Passionate about staying ahead of emerging threats, Robin focuses on developing innovative solutions to complex security challenges. He is actively developing and publishing methodologies on PredictiveDefense.io, focusing on Early Warning Intelligence and Geopolitical Cyber Threat Intelligence, aiming to provide deeper insights and stronger defenses in the ever-evolving cyber landscape.